Endorsements

I've never read a devotional that touched me as much as *Delight Yourself in the Lord...Even on Bad Hair Days*. I laughed, cried, and pondered my own life. If you buy one devotional this year, buy this one!
—**Colleen Coble**, author of the Rock Harbor series and the Mercy Falls series

* * *

Delight Yourself in the Lord...Even on Bad Hair Days will draw you closer to God even as it makes you smile and nod. The authors of this devotional know what it's like to face the difficult moments in life and to have their faith deepen because of those moments. Your faith will be deepened too.
—**Robin Lee Hatcher**, best-selling author of *Fit to Be Tied* and *A Matter of Character*

* * *

Delight Yourself in the Lord...Even on Bad Hair Days is a wonderful devotional for every woman! This book will draw you in with laughter and tears, touch your heart with the comfort and healing that only the Lord can give during those bad hair days, and remind you of what an awesome God we serve!
—**Barbara Cameron**, Hollywood mom and author of *A Full House of Growing Pains*

* * *

It is so important to renew our bodies, minds, and spirits daily. As busy women, wives, and mothers, sometimes our best intentions in caring for others can prevent us from doing just that. Time is a precious commodity for all of us. That's why I highly recommend *Delight Yourself in the Lord... Even on Bad Hair Days*. Its daily devotionals are the perfect blend of wit, wisdom, and inspiration compressed into short enough snippets that even the busiest of us can make time for. In a world where we can all use a daily reminder of hope and joy, you can be sure to find it here.
—**Julie Hadden**, from the hit NBC reality show "The Biggest Loser" and author of *Fat Chance: Losing the Weight, Gaining My Worth*

* * *

Until I read *Delight Yourself in the Lord...Even on Bad Hair Days*, I didn't know it was possible to laugh and cry at the same time while reading! Thank goodness for five funny women who are brave enough to bare their hearts—and, of course, commiserate about truly bad hair days. For me, it's an irresistible combination!
—**Shelley Shepard Gray**, author of the Seasons of Sugarcreek series

* * *

Delight Yourself in the Lord...Even on Bad Hair Days is filled with thought- and smile-provoking devotionals, penned by five of the inspirational fiction world's most successful authors. Each passage gently reminds us that we can turn to the Father for help with every big *and* little thing. I'm buying several copies to give as gifts to girlfriends who understand what bad hair days are all about!
—**Loree Lough**, award-winning author of the First Responders and Lone Star Legends series

A *Devo* for Women on the Go!

Delight Yourself
in the Lord...
Even on
Bad Hair Days

Sandra D. Bricker ✳ Kristin Billerbeck
Diann Hunt ✳ Debby Mayne ✳ Trish Perry

summerside
PRESS

Summerside Press™
Minneapolis 55438
www.summersidepress.com

Delight Yourself in the Lord...Even on Bad Hair Days
© 2010 by Kristin Billerbeck, Sandra D. Bricker, Diann Hunt,
Debby Mayne, and Trish Perry

ISBN 978-1-60936-105-1

Scripture references are from the following sources: The
Holy Bible, King James Version (KJV). The Holy Bible, New
International Version®, NIV® Copyright © 1973, 1978, 1984
by Biblica, Inc.™ Used by permission of Zondervan. All rights
reserved worldwide.

Cover and interior design by Thinkpen Graphic Design
www.thinkpendesign.com.

Cover photo © 2010 Sharon Dominick, iStockphoto

*Summerside Press™ is an inspirational publisher offering fresh,
irresistible books to uplift the heart and engage the mind.*

Printed in China.

Dedication

To our favorite warrior,
Diann Hunt.
You blessed your fellow authors and editor
with your grace and courage
as you waged your own battle with ovarian cancer
while writing these devotions.
We are so happy, humbled, and grateful
that the war is over.
Your victory is ours as well,
and we can't wait to see what
God has planned for you
on this side of the beast!

With love, admiration, and joy,
Kristin, Sandie, Debby, Trish, and Connie

Introduction

Delight yourself in the LORD,
and He will give you the desires of your heart.

PSALM 37:4

*D*on't you just love the promises God gives us in the Scriptures?
Search for me, and you'll find me. (See Jeremiah 29:13.)
I'm enough to provide you with everything you need. (See 2 Peter 1:3.)
Commit everything to me and you'll be a success. (See Proverbs 16:3.)

The promises of God form the very foundation of our faith; they say to us that, no matter what we experience, our Father is there for us and preparing a solution—or at least an escape route. Although there are times in life when this is more difficult to believe, the promises are still ours. He'll never let us down.

It is this knowledge that inspired us to write **Delight Yourself in the Lord...Even on Bad Hair Days**. The title is particularly apropos, since one of our own went through chemotherapy treatments as we worked together to write this book. Want to talk about a bad hair day?

But even in the worst of our bad hair days—or when the roof is leaking or as we receive a terrifying diagnosis or while the checking account is bouncing like a rubber ball—we know one thing for certain: delight yourself in the Lord, and He will give you the desires of your heart.

Throughout this book, it is our goal to remind our readers that joy and hope in the Lord is the opening line to every story of redemption, provision, or happily-ever-after.

With love and encouragement
from a group of women who could *curl your hair*
with stories of bad hair days!
Kristin, Sandie, Diann, Debby & Trish

Even on Bad Hair Days

Delight yourself in the LORD....

PSALM 37:4

Are you old enough to remember when Marlo Thomas's character on *That Girl* came back for a new fall season with no bangs? I don't know about you, but I was appalled!

I always identified with Ann Marie. She was the first television character that I wanted to be. During the initial season of *That Girl*, I begged my mom for bangs just like hers, but Mom wouldn't budge. So when I felt I was old enough to make hair decisions on my own, around 14, I cut them myself with a teeny pair of manicure scissors. Mom had no choice but to pretty them up, and a banged Sandie was born! I've worn them ever since, and they're an odd little part of who I am, even now.

Recently I had a particularly stellar week. I got the news that this devotional was a done deal, I had several wins on the day job, and I completed a manuscript days before it was due. In celebration, I decided to pamper myself a little. I made an appointment to get my hair cut and colored and have a relaxing facial, and I ordered Chinese takeout for dinner. Before the delivery arrived, I gave the Lord an enthusiastic shout-out, expressing my joy and gratitude for everything He'd done in my life recently.

But the Chinese food that followed sent me tumbling into a deep sleep. My dreams, I'm sorry to report, were quite tragic and filled with hair angst.

Despite the fact that just a year earlier I'd frightened my hairstylist with my reaction to her overzealous "trim" of my bangs, could the poor thing have actually had the misfortune to repeat her mistake? I sat there with my jaw in my lap, staring at my reflection in the mirror. I hadn't seen bangs that short since Julia Roberts played Tinkerbell. It was horrifying. Before I could add lyrics to the symphony of my emotions, my nervous stylist, in a desperate attempt to gloss over the damage, asked, "So, umm, what's the name of your new book?"

The question the stylist asked me just as my eyes popped open hadn't been answered. I never had the chance to tell her: *Delight Yourself in the Lord...Even on Bad Hair Days.*

But just in case the Lord was trying to tell me something through that dream, I canceled my hair appointment and rebooked with a friend's stylist, knowing full well that I would have to find a way to be "delighted" even if I walked away looking like a friend of Peter Pan. ✳ *Sandie*

Today's Prayer

Thank You for all the good hair days You afford me, Lord. And thank You for all the bad ones. No matter what I face in the mirror, on good days and bad, my hope is always in You. Amen.

Do *Not* Pull!

We love because he first loved us.

1 JOHN 4:19

If you have ever talked to a mother about how she felt when her first child was born, you'll hear words like, "I never knew I could love anyone this much."

Generally speaking, love for our children is expansive and unconditional, even when others question our devotion. Once, when...ahem!... *someone's* three sons were all under five years of age, our new church decided to have its first-ever Christmas brunch before the service to celebrate our first holiday season as a "family" with fellowship and food.

What a beautiful picture of Christ's love, right?

Now, imagine, if you will, a five-year-old boy who sees a pretty red plate on the wall and can read the sign that says DO NOT PULL. His four-year-old brother also understands the meaning of *red*. Both brothers know instinctively that, if they pull this lever, they will be in big trouble.

However, *if they talk their darling little two-year-old brother into pulling it*, that wouldn't be so bad, would it? And here's the win-win: they'd get to see what would happen and not be responsible. What could go wrong?

Just as people sat down, brunch was interrupted by the piercing wail of the fire alarm, which did not stop until the fire department arrived twenty minutes later and charged their mother $150 to turn off the alarm. And by then everyone had evacuated the first, and incidentally *the only*, Christmas brunch.

Let me just say that the organizers of this brunch were not happy. My family was not feeling the unconditional love of Christ in those moments; instead, they were feeling the consequences of sinful actions. And trust me, those boys knew what they were doing was wrong, or they wouldn't have talked their little brother into doing it for them!

Times like this inspire me to think about how God must want to drop His head into His hands at my foibles. He must think, "I know she knows better!" And He probably shakes His head and wonders if I'm ever going to get it. Just like I know that my older son's great ability to lead others can have a dark side, God knows my own weaknesses. I like to believe He cheers for me when I do the right thing and pass it on to my own children.

Sometimes the ability to love is not easy, but I think that's why God shows us what it looks like. When we see the good and the bad in others—and sometimes in ourselves—we are seeing people as God sees them: in love. Not perfect, but worthy of love. ✷ *Kristin*

Today's Prayer

Dear Jesus, thank You for creating me as You did
with a sinful nature but a heart to do rightly. Help me to find
my way in this world, to do Your will, and to forgive myself and
others as easily as You forgive me. When it's time to get up and
try again, be with me today in Your strength. Amen.

Peer Pressure—Me?

When I said, "My foot is slipping," your love, O LORD, supported me.
When anxiety was great within me, your consolation brought joy to my soul.

PSALM 94:18–19

With a husband, two kids, and twenty-eight years to my credit, I decided to go back to college. An intense Maymester course seemed to provide the perfect way to get past the speech class I'd been dreading. After all, I'd only have to endure giving speeches for four weeks instead of an entire semester.

What I hadn't counted on was getting the head of the department for a professor. Nor had I counted on ten speeches as opposed to the usual two in a normal semester (many more students, thus fewer speeches—*go figure*). And I really hadn't planned on the class debate on pornography... out on the front lawn of Purdue University...with a bullhorn...and "heckling credits."

On the day of the debate, I prepared my arguments, prayed a lot, and headed to class, ready to join the others in the fight for morality.

My adrenaline skyrocketed as I immersed myself in the heat of debate. I enjoyed the heckling (and getting free points from the professor), spouting the evils of pornography, explaining it from the perspective of a wife and a mother and, obviously, a Christian.

Then came the bottom line.

The professor called a halt to the debate. He brought us all together and drew an imaginary line in the ground. "All who are for pornography, step over here," he said. "Those who are opposed, step over there."

Imagine my surprise when the only students opposed to pornography were two guys (and forgive me, but one wore his pants up to his neck and the other spoke a different language—I have to wonder if the latter even knew what we were debating) and yours truly. The peer pressure I felt at that moment surprised me.

Class dismissed. I kicked every rock and twig from my path on my way back to the car. "Here I was trying to do the right thing. Do you know how alone I felt, Lord?"

Even as I nursed my wounds, remorse set in. The absurdity of my question rang loud and clear. Of course Jesus knew exactly how I felt. Shame choked me. I cried all the way back to the parking garage. How could I ask such a question? If anyone knew what it felt like to be alone, Jesus did. He went to the cross for me, for you...alone.

By the time I settled in the car, I realized that whatever I face in this world, He goes before me. He understands, and His grace is sufficient to get me through.

This life lesson also gave me more patience and understanding with my own children when they faced the teenage years. His consolation truly did bring joy to my soul. ✳ *Diann*

Today's Prayer

All-knowing, omnipotent Father, thank You
for understanding me even when I don't understand myself.
You are my constant joy. Amen.

Go for It…
No One's Looking

Now the serpent was more crafty than any of the wild animals
the LORD God had made. He said to the woman, "Did God really say,
'You must not eat from any tree in the garden'?"

GENESIS 3:1

From the minute I wake up until I close my eyes at night, I find myself tempted by all kinds of things I shouldn't have. Some of them are blatantly wrong for me, while others seem innocent. A convincing argument can be made for almost everything I want that I shouldn't have, and there are a lot of things I probably shouldn't have that I want.

I put myself in the place of Eve when Satan came to her in the form of a serpent. I can just imagine what that crafty little bugger would say to entice me. "Go for it…. Who'll know if you have just one little taste? No one's looking," and "What's God gonna do? Punish you just for eating a little apple?"

Um…*yeah*. Satan was the first advertising exec in the world. He not only knew his market, but he was able to strip away objections before they were even raised. He took a truth and turned it into a question, creating doubt about the status quo for his target audience. Now, I'm not saying that advertising is evil, but the temptation to tell untruths is always there …just like it is with anything. It's one thing to get the word out there about a product, but it's another to present it falsely—which is exactly what Satan did. He created doubt in Eve's mind about God's authority.

Fortunately for all humanity, God had enough love for us to override the evil from Satan by sending His Son to make us right in His eyes. How amazing is that! After Satan wreaked havoc with his false advertising campaign, he slithered away and left Adam and Eve to get themselves out of the mess he'd created. And what a mess! No way would these two mortals have been able to turn things around for the world if God hadn't fixed things.

Before my feet hit the floor in the morning, I need to immerse myself in prayer—because temptation will be around every corner and in every situation I'll face during the day. And they won't all be "obviously evil" temptations; sometimes they'll seem harmless or like the right thing to do. It's not always easy to be discerning in a work environment or even on the commute to work when someone behind you is honking, gesturing obscenely, and getting all worked up because he left five minutes later than he should have. I just have to remember God's Word and His promises to get me through. ✳ Debby

Today's Prayer

Dear Lord, make me aware of temptation as it steps
in front of me throughout the day. And give me the ability
to discern by focusing on Your Word. Amen.

Daily Miracles

Is any one of you in trouble? He should pray.
Is anyone happy? Let him sing songs of praise.
JAMES 5:13

What's the deal about praying, anyway? Why is it important to God that we pray continually, as we're told in 1 Thessalonians 5:17?

I knew a college student who kept his dog so constantly with him that they developed an uncanny level of communication. The dog understood his master's every mood and intent. The student even brought the dog with him to his classes, telling the dog to wait outside the building for him. Sure enough, the dog would settle in for the duration and be waiting when class let out. There wasn't much the student could do that the dog didn't notice.

Not to equate us with dogs, but something similar happens when we pray. The communication goes two ways, and continual prayer refines our awareness of when God answers us. We don't pray into a void. If I'm in trouble, I should tell Jesus about it. If I'm happy, I should tell Jesus about that too. I should *sing* my prayers. I should understand that my thoughts are going directly to God, not just bouncing around within my own noggin. Because not only do we communicate our needs, happiness, and every thought to God when we pray, He communicates right back. It's the *answers* we sometimes fail to recognize. And sometimes the answers are miracles. When you think of it, the very idea that God communicates with us—*that's* a miracle. I'd like to experience that and appreciate it every day.

Recently I had a sudden expenditure that took me $5,000 outside of my monthly budget. I had the money available in savings, and I reluctantly planned to withdraw that amount. But I happened to receive several small payments for some writing work I had done over the past six months, and they all came in on the same day. The amount? $5,002. Two dollars extra!

It actually took me awhile to recognize the miracle God had sent me that day, but when I did, it was like a reminder that He's aware of me, of my needs, of everything that happens in my life. As busy as He is, He notices me. He's involved.

It's not that God needs us to pray. We're the needy ones. Like that college student and his dog, if we stay constantly with Him, there won't be much He does that we won't notice. ✳ Trish

Today's Prayer

Lord Jesus, I thank You that You care so much for me
that You listen to my prayers, that You encourage me to come
to You about my troubles and my happiness. I know You answer
my prayers more often than I realize, and sometimes You answer
me with miracles. Please help me to build my connection with
You so that I recognize Your hand in what happens in my
life and in the lives of others. Amen.

Forever…That's a Mighty Long Time

"For he is the living God and he endures forever; his kingdom will not be destroyed, his dominion will never end."

Daniel 6:26

Time is a hard concept for me. The image of forever? Almost impossible to fathom. My day is cut into tiny chunks. Work has to be scheduled into time slots between dropping off kids for school, soccer, and playdates; dinner; laundry; homework; doctors' appointments; and the rest. Work is actually a luxury—and it leaves me thinking, how did I get here?

Life was meant to be savored, enjoyed, but the reality of day to day gets in the way of that. It's easy to think about God in terms of "He'll be there later. I'll get to Him." But the Bible tells us to seek *first* His kingdom and all shall be added. I've found that to be true—that if I give God the first part of my day, He will honor the rest by making me more productive and better able to function with all that's on my schedule that day.

But forever… What could I do with forever?

Sometimes I think the only thing I want to do with forever is sit down! With three boys, that kind of forever just doesn't happen. It's then that I need to remember God's version of forever—eternity…that the small things in life matter, they make up the whole. Sure, furniture comes and goes, socks are lucky if they make it through the first washing, and don't even get me started on the groceries that barely seem to make it into the house, but if we can take that time to focus on God's version of forever, the daily tasks are easier.

God only asks for a small portion of our day. In return, He gives us forever. Isn't that huge? It's like us asking our kids to do their homework and pick up their socks. In return, we'll give them three square meals a day, an education, a roof over their heads, and clean underpants. It's not a bad deal. So they should take it, right? Well, I should too, but all too often, I'm guilty of getting busy first and crying out to God for relief next.

When I think of eternity, I love to picture a ring, because it is without end. God loves us without end, but wouldn't it be nice if we engraved something on that ring this morning? What if we told God how much He means to us or how much He gives us while He expects so little in return? ✳ *Kristin*

Today's Prayer

Dear Jesus, thank You for each day You give us here on earth. Help me to honor You in the early moments of my day and prepare for all You have given me to tackle. Calm my heart and help me to remember that You are in charge. You have ordained all that I have to manage, and I need only to be reminded that you are there—ready to help. In Your holy name, amen.

The Definition of a Really Bad Day

A cheerful heart is good medicine,
but a crushed spirit dries up the bones.

PROVERBS 17:22

My mom and I had a bad period that lasted from the time I was a teenager until my late thirties. We found ways to butt heads in very creative ways, even when thousands of miles stretched between us. Then she became ill, and I made a decision that was either going to bridge the considerable gap between us...or it was going to explode in my face. I moved from Los Angeles to Tampa to provide care for her.

My mom and I bonded in awesome ways during those few years after I moved to Florida. Oh, make no mistake, we still butted heads. However, I had the opportunity to get to know her, woman to woman, and I really fell in love with her. We forged out a second relationship where she was *Mom* again, and I was the child who adored her.

When she passed away, the grief was just about the most profound mountain I've ever faced. Sitting in the limousine behind the hearse carrying her casket, my emotions took the shape of a tsunami threatening in the distance. I had no idea how I would cope with walking into that church and saying good-bye to this woman who had unexpectedly (and miraculously) become my closest friend.

Please, Lord. Help me. I can't take it.

A car cut in front of the hearse, and the hearse's driver slammed on the brakes, as did the driver of the limousine carrying my brother and me. In that moment of recovery afterward, something phenomenal happened.

I started to giggle. Softly at first...and then I tumbled into full-fledged laughter as I remembered a particular moment with my mom.

Munching popcorn and watching one of those really awful movies on television on a Saturday afternoon, the film plot involved a hearse with squealing brakes followed by the back doors opening and the casket sliding out and thumping to a stop in the middle of the road. My mom turned to me and said, "Now *that* is the definition of a really bad day."

Everyone in the funeral limo looked at me as if I'd lost my mind. I tried to explain myself, but the laughter rolling out of me challenged the effort.

By the time I reached the church, my dried and crushed spirit had been revived, soothed over with the balm of a cheerful heart. An unlikely healing had been brought about by a single memory and ten solid minutes of subsequent, almost uncontrollable, laughter. ✽ *Sandie*

Today's Prayer

Lord, thank You for Your healing power, both in my
relationships and in my emotions. Help me to remember
today that laughter can be a powerful balm to the heart.
Remind me to never take myself or my situation so
seriously that it buries me and hides the promise
that, yes, I will laugh again. Amen.

Stage Fright

"Now go; I will help you speak and will teach you what to say."

EXODUS 4:12

People who know me well may be surprised to find out what an intro-vert I truly am. With close friends, I can be myself and let go of my insecurities and shortcomings, resulting in a gregarious side that mere acquaintances never see.

Consequently, as a result of my shyness, when my first book came out and I had a scheduled radio interview, I began to sweat. A lot.

On that fateful day, my heart thumped hard against my chest with every tick of the clock. The countdown was on as I waited for the call. How could I talk about my first book? I'd moved on to writing other books and could barely remember what I had written in the first one. What if I drew a blank? Hey, it happens to menopausal women. Trust me. I know this from personal experience. I prayed and ransacked the house in search of chocolate.

I wanted this interview to be about the book, about the Lord's faith-fulness, not about me. But I was at the interviewer's mercy. The questions she shot at me would be answered off-the-cuff.

I don't *do* "off-the-cuff."

The time came and passed. No phone call. My stomach coiled and rolled. Still no phone call. It occurred to me that someone might have told her about my phobia with interviews. I prayed she'd call soon—I was quickly slipping into a chocolate coma.

An hour or so later, the interviewer called. She apologized for being late. She'd had chemotherapy that morning and was running behind. What? *Chemotherapy?* I was worrying about a silly interview while she was dealing with chemotherapy?

All fear left me.

My heart ached to know how to console her in her journey. We discussed her situation and how God was getting her through. We even laughed together. By the time we got to the actual interview, I wasn't the least bit nervous. We had bonded over something far more important than a book review. We were "sisters in the faith," traveling an uncertain road, with the Lord by our side.

As I forgot *myself*, the Lord gave me the words to encourage my sister. My concern for her made me forget the less important matters. I never had to consider where my words would come from; they were just there because He was there, to heal, encourage, and strengthen—both of us.

So whether you have a radio interview or a coffee meeting with a neighbor, keep your eyes fixed on Jesus. He will give you the words to say, and His words make all the difference. ✳ Diann

Today's Prayer

Yahweh, how I love when You arrange appointments for me. Thank You for giving me the words to speak when I step away from my comfort zone. Thank You for Your constant guidance.

There's No Place Like Home

Lord, you have been our dwelling place throughout all generations.

PSALM 90:1

I let out a deep sigh as I turned onto my street after conducting an all-day workshop with three other authors. The weeks of planning showed, and the day had been a success, but I was exhausted—and I couldn't wait to kick off my shoes, get out of my business clothes, and slip into some shorts and a T-shirt.

My preparation for the day involved more than the workshop. I'd spent a couple of afternoons organizing and cleaning so I could walk back into my tidy house after the workshop and relax. With weary enthusiasm, I shoved the key into the lock, turned it, and pushed open the door. The instant I took my first step inside, I felt like the floor had fallen out from beneath me.

I blinked, hoping it was a bad dream, but it wasn't. As I looked around, I saw toilet paper strewn from one side of the house to the other. One living room lamp lay on its side, and the other one was leaning haphazardly against the wall.

My husband and daughters had been gone all day and they still weren't back, so there was no one to blame but my dog and two cats, all of them lined up and looking at me with fake innocence. I narrowed my eyes and glared at them. If they'd had opposable thumbs, I would have ordered them to help me clean up.

I numbly made my way to my bedroom, glancing at the kitchen on the way—where I saw an even bigger mess. An empty, ripped bread bag hung over the edge of the counter. The trash can lay on its side, with coffee grounds smeared over the brand-new tile floor and smooshed into the grout that I hadn't yet sealed. Obviously, the cats and dog had tag-teamed.

"Bad dog," I mumbled as I backed away from the mess. "Bad kitties." I went into my bedroom that I'd thankfully remembered to close off to the animals, dropped my handbag onto the bed, and changed into something comfortable to clean up the mess. Instead of relaxing like I'd hoped, I went on a cleaning frenzy to straighten up my home and work off the frustration. As I cleaned, I thought about the messes I've made in life and how God's sacrifice was much greater than mine. The perspective quickly cooled me down.

My husband and daughters arrived home shortly after I finished getting everything back into shape. The girls flopped onto the sofa to watch TV, while my husband joined me in the kitchen. "So how was your day?" he asked. "Did the workshop go well?" ✳ *Debby*

Today's Prayer

Thank You, Lord, for providing shelter for me while I'm here in this world. Help me to stay focused on my eternal life with You in the place You have prepared in Your mansion in heaven. Amen.

You Needed Me

*"And who knows but that you have come
to royal position for such a time as this?"*

ESTHER 4:14

One of my best friends lost her husband to cancer a few years ago. Matt was a sweetheart, but he wasn't a believer until it was almost too late. God was patient with him, though, and so was his wife, Val. Their marriage was no cakewalk (what marriage is?), and Matt's lack of interest in salvation couldn't have been easy for Val to accept. Had I been in her shoes, I think I would have henpecked for Jesus, and we all know how effective that is. But Val carried on as a believer, a churchgoer, a women's Bible study leader, and most importantly for her husband, an ever-patient wife who evangelized by example.

Very shortly before his death, Matt quietly accepted the Lord into his heart. Obviously, that event brought great comfort to Val in the midst of her grief after he died.

As she drove around town running errands several months later, the old Anne Murray song "You Needed Me" came on the radio. Although Val had always loved the song, the lyrics were especially poignant to her now and reminded her of how much she had needed Matt in her life. He had wiped away her tears and given her strength and held her when she was cold. Despite the conflicts they'd experienced in their life together, Val realized what a gift God had given her, to create Matt for such a time as that he spent with her. And she felt God blessed her at that moment in her car, to draw her attention to a song suggesting what Matt had done for her.

Oddly, the next day the old song came on again. After years of not playing, it played for Val two days in a row. "Okay, Lord," she said, "what are You trying to show me?" And it was as if the lyrics changed to remind her of what she had done for Matt by representing Christ to him all those years. The lyrics spoke about the buying back of one's soul, about turning lies into truth, about putting one on a pedestal high enough that he could see eternity. She understood she had been created for such a time as that she spent with Matt. Again, God blessed her then by drawing her attention to a song suggesting what He had done for Matt and how she had been His instrument.

As believers, we're all His instruments, whether we realize it or not. He puts each of us in "royal positions" for specific moments in time. It's up to us to seek our purpose and to serve Him well. Who knows? Maybe today you'll fulfill His purpose for you. ✳ *Trish*

Today's Prayer

Lord Jesus, I'm honored to play a role
in Your plans. Help me to recognize that role
and to represent You well. Amen.

No Pain, No Gain

A happy heart makes the face cheerful,
but heartache crushes the spirit.

PROVERBS 15:13

*H*ave you ever walked through the valley of the shadow of death? Really been heartsick over what life has dealt? I've been there, and sometimes a Bible verse can be wielded at you like a weapon, not as one to give one hope. Oh, sure, people mean well, but we cannot go through our dark times next to people who tell us we deserve it. *Uh, I think you wanted Job's house next door, thanks.*

I was twenty-nine when I was diagnosed with multiple sclerosis. I'd gone blind one night; my eyes were jumping like the vertical hold on an old TV gone bad. Being an optimist, I was determined to fight this with everything I had. But to get my eyesight back, the "cure" was steroids via infusion followed by a long, tapering dose of more steroids.

These aren't the pretty steroids that make you bulky and muscular. No, these make you plump like a Ball Park hot dog, morph your face into a shade of violet blueberry, and, as an added bonus, give you acne like you've hit puberty. I still cannot stand to see pictures of myself during that time because I remember how sick I felt, how utterly lacking in energy I was.

During that time, I tried the MS "diet," exercise, and having my church anoint me with oil and pray for me. One day at church, a complete stranger came up to me and said, "You have MS because you have unconfessed sin in your life."

Honestly, my first thought was, "So do you. Why aren't you sick?"

Something about that statement, however, freed me to really trust that God was with me through all this. It gave me a cheerful heart because I laughed at the ridiculousness of walking up to a total stranger and saying something so negative. I wish now I'd said, "Hey, that's helpful. How about if you bring a meal over on Tuesday, oh prophetic one?"

There are always things that will bring you down in this lifetime: sickness, death, breakups, losing your job. Some days you won't feel like laughing, and that's okay. King Solomon said, "Sorrow is better than laughter, because a sad face is good for the heart" (Ecclesiastes 7:3).

It's been fifteen years since I first went blind, and I haven't had that kind of attack since. I'm still walking—running, on a good day—still driving. I'm still working through the symptoms of MS, but I don't regret it for a moment. The sadness of being sick gave me more compassion. It taught me that sometimes we have to lean on others and, most importantly, it made me appreciate good health. ✳ *Kristin*

Today's Prayer

Dear Jesus, thank You for giving us emotions, both the good
and the bad, so that we might appreciate that You are with us
in them all. May my heart be filled with gratitude and joy today.

We Are Family

*But Ruth replied, "Don't urge me to leave you or to turn back from you.
Where you go I will go, and where you stay I will stay. Your people
will be my people and your God my God. Where you die I will die,
and there I will be buried."*

RUTH 1:16–17

My friend Jemelle is always the coolest person in the room. She's beautiful; she's straight-out-there, in-your-face direct; and she's a closet comedienne. I like to say she's a Hollywood A-Lister on the outside with the heart of a true Southern belle.

That's how I describe her *now*. When I met her on the first day of training for the only job I could find when I left California and moved to Florida, it was a completely different story.

I was out of my element, insecure about my new surroundings and feeling a little deflated about the turn my life had taken. I'm sure that had something to do with my perception that *Miss Thing* had judged me as *The Loser* in the room. I had no interest in getting to know her, but in that way God often has of moving us around like chess pieces so an opportunity can present itself, we just kept crossing paths. And it didn't take long for me to realize how wrong I'd been.

My mom's death closed the door on *family* for me, but Jemelle started including me in her holiday celebrations. For Christmas Eve festivities, Easter dinners, the obligatory Southern tradition of black-eyed peas on New Year's Day, I'm at the Nelson-Tola family table. When I feel the most alone, confused, or frightened, Jemelle is one of the first people I call. When something wonderful happens, she's who I want to tell. She doesn't always say what I hope she will, but most of the time she is my soft place to fall when I need one the most. I adore her parents, Dot and Bud, and they've embraced me into the fold without hesitation.

Jemelle and her amazing husband adopted a little girl and named her Olivia. A year after that, they brought Nico home. Just as they opened their arms and offered family warmth to me when my blood ties had dissolved, Jemelle and Alberto wanted to give two more lost souls a soft place of their own. In the same way that the blood of Jesus grafts us all into His family, these children became grafted extensions of the family that means so much to me. And as Ruth said to Naomi, I say to Jemelle, "Don't urge me to leave you....Your people will be my people." ✳ Sandie

Today's Prayer

Lord Jesus, thank You so much for thinking of me
when setting up the seating arrangement for the party.
Knowing that each deep connection in my life was inspired
by You, help me to keep my eyes open for the role I can
play in the lives of others to pay it forward. Amen.

Give Thanks in All Circumstances

Be joyful always; pray continually; give thanks in all circumstances,
for this is God's will for you in Christ Jesus.

1 THESSALONIANS 5:16–18

There are many things I can deal with in this life, but a face without eyebrows? Can I be honest here? I'm *so* not thankful for that. A bald head? We can cover that with a turban or wig. No eyelashes? Use eyeliner. No eyebrows? "Houston, we've got a problem."

Chemotherapy has brought new meaning to the phrase "blank expression." On a side note, I walked into the kitchen the other day, forgetting that my eyebrows weren't penciled in yet, and my husband saw me for the first time, eyebrow-less. The surprise in his eyes provoked an immediate response. I lifted my hand in the Star Trek sign and said in a robotic voice, "Mmmm, I am from the Planet Votar."

Call me vain, but I want eyebrows. Yes, there are worse things in life than not having eyebrows, but in my fifty-four years, I've grown rather attached to them.

Still, I have to admit that it's a challenge to draw on eyebrows. Try it sometime. You'll see what I mean. My sweet husband tried to help when he bought me some eyebrow stencils, but they were thick—Groucho Marx thick. I would have needed a Magic Marker to fill them in. Not exactly the look I was going for. The worst part of drawing on my eyebrows is that I have a problem with keeping my hands off my face. I talk with my hands.

What? Lots of people do that, don't they?

Unfortunately, that means my hands are constantly touching my face. I never realized how much I did this until one day, over lunch, when I told a story and wiped out an entire eyebrow before I'd finished my salad.

Give thanks in all circumstances? It occurs to me that the important word in that phrase is not the "all," but rather the "in." I'm not giving thanks *for* my circumstances, but rather *in* them. While I am in the midst of these circumstances, I give Jesus thanks *for who He is*. I can be thankful "in" my life's circumstances, knowing that God is in control; He loves me. He is my joy and my constant companion.

And the truth is, I can actually give thanks for the eyebrow problem, because it has helped me to laugh along this journey. You may have a bad hair day, I may have a bad eyebrow day, but all in all, it's a downright good day. Because the way I see it, anything that makes me laugh with the joy of Jesus is a good day. A very good day. ✳ *Diann*

Today's Prayer

Father, I can be joyful always and give thanks in all circumstances when You are in control of my life. Help me to remember that there is nothing I will face today that I can't get through with You by my side. Amen.

Don't Rush Me

The Lord is not slow in keeping his promise,
as some understand slowness. He is patient with you,
not wanting anyone to perish, but everyone to come to repentance.

2 PETER 3:9

"C'mon, Lauren, get the lead out," I remember telling my younger daughter, who had to do one more thing before leaving for school. "They're not gonna wait for you, ya know."

"I'm coming," she said. "Just don't rush me. I'll be on time." I stormed to my car and sat there tapping my fingertips on the steering wheel, fuming, and wondering why I always had to wait for her—or anyone for that matter. It seemed like I was the only person who ever looked at a clock and took my time commitments seriously.

Lauren finally came out to the car, carrying her books in one hand and her shoes in the other, with her bag slung over her shoulder. During the fifteen-minute drive to school, she put on her shoes, finished applying her makeup, and checked to make sure she had all her homework. We were halfway to the school when she let out a soft groan. "I left the most important thing on the dining room table," she said. "Can you bring it to me before second period?"

I made some noise but finally agreed to bring it to her. After all, she was in high school, and I didn't want this one homework assignment to keep her out of college. So I dropped her off, rushed home, grabbed her paper, and went back to the school, where I left her assignment with the administrative assistant at the front desk.

The rest of my day was just as frantic, so by the time everyone came back home, I was a mess. My husband gave me a sidelong glance. "You seem out of sorts. What happened?" That was all it took to get me started.

I told him how I'd felt "behind the eight ball" all day. "Just because Lauren forgot her homework?" he asked, shaking his head.

Uh...yeah. "It threw me behind by at least a half hour."

"Do you think maybe you're doing too much?" He wasn't being sarcastic. He really wanted to know. I've been a freelance writer for a very long time, and most of my schedule was self-imposed. But still...

I guess by now it must be clear that I'm not the most patient person in the world. Second Peter 3:9 is a prime example of why I need to work on that. The Lord loves each and every one of us, and He's exercising patience before returning to save us for eternity. I definitely need to follow His lead. ✱ *Debby*

Today's Prayer

Dear Jesus, help me to learn by Your example
in every aspect of my journey in this world. I pray that
I can learn to be more patient and understanding
with all the people You bring into my life. Amen.

A Love Eternally There

In my anguish I cried to the LORD, and he answered by setting me free.

PSALM 118:5

nyone who has experienced the joy of taking wedding vows knows how it goes: "I, [your name], take you, [his name], to be my lawfully wedded husband, to have and to hold from this day forward, for better or worse, for richer or poorer, in sickness and in health, to love and to cherish, from this day forward, until death do us part. And if things don't work out, I will be out of there so fast, my dust will blind you, buddy boy."

Uh, no. I don't know a divorced Christian woman anywhere who married with the attitude that things might not work out. Love is awesome! And Christians commit to forever. But sometimes no matter how committed we are, marriage *doesn't* work out. If yours has, you know you're blessed. If yours hasn't, you're not alone. Sometimes spouses surprise us with alcoholism, abuse, or attraction to what just ain't right. Sometimes we come home to a terse note and an empty closet.

When I came home to such a situation, I went into a bit of shock. After sixteen years of marriage—every one of which was a struggle—I scrambled to figure out how life would ever be manageable again. I prayed. I called my best friend. I opened the local paper to find out just how unemployable I had become for having trusted that God wanted me to be a stay-at-home mom. But one thing I absolutely did not do? I did not turn against God.

God was my absolute rock all through my troubled marriage. I knew my heart was a huge part of the problem. I knew my husband's heart was the other huge part of the problem. But God? He was rooting for healing the entire time. He would have loved and rewarded complete surrender from the two of us. He didn't get it.

That's a scary place for a separated wife to be: feeling like her husband left out of extreme disappointment in her...and wondering if God was equally disappointed. How far away will *He* go?

In my fear, I cried out to Him. I was hurt; I was panicked; I was anxious about the future. And most of all, I thought He might just turn His back on *me*.

Perhaps you're in that place right now. Or maybe someone you know is in that place and she needs your support and prayers. Tell her—or tell yourself—that calling on Him is absolutely necessary and fruitful. He will uphold you. He will protect you. He will set you free. ✳ *Trish*

Today's Prayer

Lord, whatever role I played in my troubles today,
I know You still love me. Help me to see what I must do
to make it through each day. I know that, as always,
I can do nothing to earn the gift of love
You have never taken away. Amen.

Chasing Dreams and Chasing Tails

He who pursues righteousness and love finds life, prosperity and honor.

PROVERBS 21:21

It's almost impossible to describe the drastic changes that took place in daily reality while living in the Silicon Valley during the tech boom. Companies were giving away BMWs to young engineers who signed on to work for them. Money appeared to be rolling in, hand over fist, for anyone who had an idea. The venture capitalists couldn't seem to give it away fast enough, and millions were made in a stock bubble that would eventually come to an end.

During this time, we had many friends who became filthy rich. As a family, we did well too, but we had friends moving into multimillion-dollar estates, buying luxury cars with cash, and sending their kids to elite private schools. If that isn't a perfect picture for how we, as God's children, become so entitled, I'm not sure what is.

It is such a natural thing to take that wealth and pursue something bigger and better (we ourselves got a fabulous built-in pool). If we take our eyes off the prize, it is so easy to pursue that which really doesn't make our lives any more fulfilled, our families any happier, or give our lives any great purpose. More stuff equals more earthly things to take care of and, ultimately, sucks the joy from one's life. After all, we're told not to build up our treasures on earth, where thieves can break in and steal them, but to build treasures in heaven.

We watched families self-destruct over the pursuit of money, over the love of work before family, over a complete lack of connection. Interestingly, the strongest couples some ten years later are those who gained nothing from the tech boom except a striking look at reality.

Having money is not a sin. The *love of money* is a sin, and I think it's so easy to get focused on what we don't have when others seem to have it all. But you can be happy right here, in the midst of whatever struggle God has given you today. You can pursue righteousness and love and live a life of prosperity and honor, no matter what your current situation.

As a witness to the testimony that money does not make you happy, ask yourself the serious question of what does make you happy. More connection? More family time? More nights out with the girls? More teaching? More serving?

God can quiet your heart. He can meet your needs, and He wants you to prosper where He has you planted. Look for your joys and your blessings, and pursue who God made you to be. ✳ *Kristin*

Today's Prayer

Dear Jesus, help me to focus on today and what You want
from me in this moment. You created me for a special purpose;
help me to understand what that is, and when I get off track,
gently push me back where I belong. In His name, amen.

I Wanna Bend It Like Bailey

But seek first his kingdom and his righteousness,
and all these things will be given to you as well.

MATTHEW 6:33

I adore children, and my favorite age is right around three or four; they're just developing their communications skills but haven't quite perfected the transition from emotion to verbalization.

While babysitting for a friend's three-year-old, I encountered the challenge of keeping Bailey occupied so that she might forget that her beloved mommy had left the house without her. And it wasn't easy.

First, we played Safari. After strategically placing her most treasured stuffed animals around the house, Bailey put on a plastic pith helmet and climbed aboard her push-and-ride Jeep, and we toured the African plains of home to observe the animals in their natural habitat. When she spotted the giraffe leaning against the refrigerator, Bailey suddenly remembered who had given her that giraffe, and she started to cry for her mother.

Several games and a coloring book later, she accepted my invitation to a tea party in her bedroom. We donned straw hats, and Bailey tugged on little white crocheted gloves. Along with two of our very best doll friends, we sipped from empty teacups and munched imaginary scones with cream and strawberries. Bailey was enthralled!...*until the garage door went up*. Tossing the plastic teacup to the floor, she flew from the bedroom and down the hall. On her trail, I stepped over the hat and the gloves she'd shed on the way. I reached her just as the kitchen door opened and her mother walked in.

So excited to see her mom again at last, Bailey squealed with glee. When the words wouldn't come, she finally began hopping from one foot to the other, pumping her arms, clenching her fists, and contorting her little face. The return of her mother had trumped everything else, and thoughts of tea parties and safaris had fallen to the dust. I stood there watching as the child completely surrendered to the ecstatic happiness of seeing the one person who meant more to her than anything or anyone else.

On the drive home that afternoon, I tuned my radio to a local Christian station playing "I Can Only Imagine" by MercyMe, a song exploring the depths of our reaction when we finally see Christ face-to-face. As I sang along, Bailey's reaction to her mother's return home sprang to mind. How sweet would it be to the Lord if, at His presence, we just jumped up and down with the glee of little children! ✳ *Sandie*

Today's Prayer

Oh Lord, thank You for the sweet parenthood You offer us.
Let me always see You as Abba Father, through enthusiastic
and childlike eyes. Today I am overcome with joy as I delight
myself in You, remembering that Your arms always welcome
me, Your thoughts are always about my well-being, and
there is no one else I would rather see. Amen.

True Thirst

O God, you are my God, earnestly I seek you; my soul thirsts for you,
my body longs for you, in a dry and weary land where there is no water.

PSALM 63:1

Food and drink have no control over me whatsoever. Absolutely none. At least that's what I thought until they told me I had to "fast" for twelve hours before a medical test.

It's not as though I am a stranger to fasting. I have fasted many times for matters of prayer and drawing closer to the Lord but, admittedly, it has been a while. Funny how the passing of time can change things.

What was it about knowing I couldn't have something that made me want it all the more? The minute they told me I couldn't have anything to eat, I was starving. No drink? These were medical people. Didn't they realize I could get dehydrated?

By the morning, my mouth was so dry that my lips stuck to my gums and refused to cover my teeth. Lovely mental picture, huh? Coffee called out my name with the lure of a half-price sale at Macy's. I resisted—but not without attitude.

The thing was, I could skip the food, the drink, all that, if I didn't know I had to. It was the knowing I *had* to do it that made me feel as though I'd been walking through a desert for days without food or drink. The air smelled of chocolate, and every billboard seemed to tease my senses and heighten my need for nourishment.

Which brings to mind my next question: have I ever longed for Jesus in the same way? So hungry, so thirsty for Him that I can think of nothing else? Does He consume me to the point that my spiritual hunger and thirst will not be quenched until I spend time with Him?

I heard a story once where a man asked his friend how he could truly find God. The friend took the man to a nearby lake, and once they were shoulder-deep in the water, he said, "You're sure you *truly* want to find God?"

The man answered, "Yes."

So the friend dunked the man in the water and held his head down to the point where the man thought he would drown. When the friend pulled him back up, the man gasped, coughed, and sputtered, all the while desperately trying to pull air into his burning lungs.

Finally the friend said, "When you want to find God as much as you desired your breath, you will find Him."

I'm not sure where this story originated, but I heard it years ago and never forgot it. As much as I long to know God more, I've never longed for him with that kind of desperation.

Have you? ✴ *Diann*

Today's Prayer

Amazing Lord of all creation, as the daily grind
of life consumes me, help me to remember that
You are the very air that I breathe. Amen.

Who's That Lady?

"At least there is hope for a tree: If it is cut down,
it will sprout again, and its new shoots will not fail."

JOB 14:7

After months of having my hair tugged and yanked by my firstborn, Alison, I decided to get it chopped off. I didn't have a babysitter who could watch her during the week, so I waited until the weekend when my husband, Wally, would be with us. We decided to take a family trip to the mall, where he agreed to window-shop with Alison while I went to the hair salon. It took about an hour, start to finish, and when I walked out of the salon, I was excited to show off my new 'do to my family.

I eagerly watched the main corridor of the mall until I spotted my husband and baby coming out of a store. My heart thudded as they got closer. I practically ran toward them until I was close enough to reach for my baby. The second I touched Alison, her eyes widened, a panicked look came over her chubby little face, and she let out an ear-piercing scream. It took a few seconds before I understood what had happened. *She didn't recognize me.* Some strange woman with short hair was grabbing at her, and she didn't like it a bit.

For the next couple of hours I talked to her, and Wally did his best to explain that I was still "Mommy," only with shorter hair. She stared at me dubiously, but she kept pulling back when I so much as touched her. It took time until, finally, she accepted the new "Mommy"—but I could tell by the way she looked at me, she didn't care for what she saw.

As Alison grew, so did my hair, and thankfully she'd gotten out of the habit of grabbing it. Although I enjoyed the shorter cut for a while, I'd always had longer hair, so I was glad to have it at least shoulder-length again.

Like my hair, after a tree is cut, it continues to grow unless it is pulled up by its roots—then it will die. After we pass away, we won't return to this earth in our current condition. I decide what happens with my hair—whether it is short or long. But our life after death is up to the Lord, and He has made it clear that through faith in Him, we will be with Him eternally. Trees need nourishment that they get from the soil, water, and sun. In order to keep my faith alive and healthy, I need to read my Bible and study His Word. ✱ *Debby*

Today's Prayer

Keep me nourished by Your Word, Jesus, so that I may stay alive with You forever. I pray that my faith will bloom and that You will use me to help plant the seed of faith in others. Amen.

I'll Be a Fool for You

Fear of man will prove to be a snare,
but whoever trusts in the LORD is kept safe.

PROVERBS 29:25

several years ago, a friend of mine heard from her sister-in-law, Kerry, who was absolutely floored about something. She had been running errands when she stopped at a convenience store for a soda. As she walked in, she felt the profound presence of God and was certain she heard Him instruct her to go to the back of the store and stand on her head.

I'm not making this up. But, honestly, what would *you* have done? I'm not sure I'm coordinated enough to even attempt a headstand, let alone worry about how foolish I'd look.

This dear sister in Christ, though, fought the fear of what others would think, and in total trust of God's will, did exactly as she felt she was divinely instructed. Within seconds, a female employee walked out of the store's back room, took one look at Kerry, screamed, and started babbling almost incoherently.

Kerry immediately righted herself and took the crying woman in hand. Apparently the employee, a borderline atheist, had given up on her lonely, difficult life. She'd been in the back room crying and contemplating the worst. In the midst of her depression, she called out to God. She had never been able to accept His existence or believe He loved her because the pain in her life seemed too bad to coexist with a loving God. Still, in her desperation she shared her anger with Him.

"I'll tell you what," she cried, "I'll believe You exist when I walk out of here and see someone standing on their head." Then she walked out of the back room and into the kingdom.

Now, if God put it into my head that there was someone contemplating suicide who would change her mind about Him and about life if I would only stand on my head in the middle of a convenience store, I'd surely put aside my fear of what others might think. I'd probably even recruit someone to help me get myself upside down. But to "hear" the instructions Kerry heard and obey without knowing why? I think I'd have to hear them like Charlton Heston heard the burning bush. I'd need to be *very* certain before I'd trust that what I "heard" was the Lord before setting aside the possible embarrassment of misunderstanding. That's the "fear of man" referred to in today's verse.

Joshua marched around Jericho. Gideon dismissed all but three hundred men before taking on the Midianite hordes. Jesus's adoptive father, Joseph, married a girl his contemporaries might have stoned. How loudly would you need to hear His voice before it would drown out the judgment of your fellow man? ✳ Trish

Today's Prayer

Lord, help me to hear Your voice today and always.
Help me to fear and trust You more than I fear what
people will think because I obeyed You. Amen.

Justice Feels Good

When David heard that Nabal was dead, he said, "Praise be to the LORD, who has upheld my cause against Nabal for treating me with contempt. He has kept his servant from doing wrong and has brought Nabal's wrongdoing down on his own head."

1 SAMUEL 25:39

Let's face it, a just sentence feels good. If it didn't, the Lifetime Movie Network would be out of business. There would be no abyss-falling villains at the end of Disney movies, and there would certainly be no Court TV. When the unrighteous get theirs and we get to witness it, there's a certain satisfaction that comes over us as humans. As much as we'd like to be pious and beyond such pettiness, it secretly feels good to watch evil perish. Especially if we've seen the victims of its wrath suffer.

I admit it; this is why I love the story of Abigail in the Bible. She was married to an idiot. Nabal's name actually means "foolish," and worse than being a fool, he was a fool for no purpose—other than to be contrary and show his power. He might have sacrificed his entire family and all his servants for the opportunity to exert his rights over David and not give David and his men a few of his flock. Out of his foolishness came pure wickedness.

Fearing that her household and her children would perish over Nabal's decision, Abigail defied her husband and humbly appeared before David with supplies and an apology on behalf of Nabal's behavior. She asked David to remember her when he was able.

Abigail, being a smart wife, waited until morning after Nabal had slept off his drink to tell him of her actions. Rather than being grateful for being alive, Nabal was struck like a stone and died ten days later.

Now, I'm not wishing anyone dead. I'm only saying that, when the right man gets his, there's such a beauty in earthly justice. Abigail's fortitude and humility saved the lives of many. Not only that, but David returned for her later and asked her to be his wife. A vast improvement after Nabal, I'm certain.

I love this story of how a woman put her faith in God and defied evil. Naturally, we don't always get to see God's justice here on earth, but we can remember God's love for us when all feels lost. ✳ *Kristin*

Today's Prayer

Dear Jesus, this morning, I pray that I would hear
Your righteous voice in my ear, that I would do the best thing for
You and for all the people You have entrusted me to look after.
When I feel all hope is lost, remind me that You hate evil so
much more than I am capable of—and that Your will should be
done here on earth as it is in heaven. Amen.

It's a Dog's Life

For God is not a God of disorder but of peace.

1 CORINTHIANS 14:33

Iadopted my sheepdog Caleb when he was barely a year old, and he died at sixteen from bone cancer. I knew I stood no chance of forging a connection like that with an animal again. After all, Caleb had taken me through my own cancer before I accompanied him on his battle, and we'd been best buddies, constant companions.

When I met Sophie at Rescue Day in the parking lot of the pet supply store, the first thing I noticed in her eyes (behind unmistakable fear) was a strange sort of recognition. She looked at me as if she'd spotted an old friend. I heard stories about her past that broke my heart, and the skittish little red-haired collie struck me as a very different dog than my Caleb. Still, I wanted to give her a home.

On our first night together, she slept in the hallway outside my bedroom, watching me from a distance. When the time came for lights-out, our eyes met for a long moment, and I patted the bed, inviting her to join me—but she crossed her paws and laid her head on them. About two hours later, however, I opened my eyes and found her standing next to the bed, her ears cocked as she stared at me.

"What's wrong?" I asked. She took a step backward then surprised me as she jumped up on the bed beside me. I set my hand on her head and stroked her pointed ears as I said a prayer over her. She looked up at me gratefully when I was through, staring into my eyes with such profound emotion.

"I can promise you this," I told her in a whisper. "I'll never hurt you, and I'll take very good care of you. I know how much discord there's been in your life up to now, but this is a house of peace. You'll be safe here. If we learn to love one another along the way, all the better."

There hasn't been a single night since then that Sophie hasn't curled up beside me. Often she waits for the very instant that I sit down on the bed, and she'll hop up and toss herself into my lap with complete, trusting abandon. Sophie and I have indeed learned to love one another, and I think we provide reciprocal peace that we both value beyond measure. It wasn't until recently, several years into our relationship, that I realized I'd heard those same words spoken to me once upon a time. The Lord had invited me to rest with Him and promised me I would find peace in His arms, just as Sophie had found peace in mine. ✻ Sandie

Today's Prayer

Lord, thank You for blessing me with Your love, peace, and strong sense of family. Help me always to pass it on to others.

I Know Your Name

*And the Lord said to Moses, "I will do the very thing you have asked,
because I am pleased with you and I know you by name."*

EXODUS 33:17

I can't remember names. It's as though I've missed out on some kind of memory gene or something. I've gone to church with people for years whose names, when push comes to shove, just don't come to mind.

At one book signing, a woman I knew came up and bought a book of mine. She was from my church, but her name was buried deep within a dust-covered file at the back of my brain, and it refused to open. I could have gotten by, exchanging a few pleasantries, but when she bought my book and asked me to sign it, I knew I was in trouble.

I used the standard line I use when I forget a name. With a smile, I looked at her and said, "Since people spell their names differently, I'd better ask how you spell yours." Perspiration popped out on my forehead as the clock ticked in her silence.

"Jan," she said in a voice void of emotion. "J–A–N." She left a long pause between each letter.

Okay, so I'm slow, but I'm not that slow.

"Kind of hard to misspell that one," I said with a nervous laugh.

I have no idea what happened after that. I can't remember. However, you can rest easy about one thing. I'll never forget her name again. At least, I don't think I will.

Believe me, I work on this problem. I've tried using the method where you remember something on a person's face with the idea that it will give you a clue to their name. But when I look at them, I think, *Was it that mole on her cheek that was supposed to tell me something? Her green eyes? The unibrow?* I get so off track, the name gets dumped in an empty corner and white noise fills my head.

These scenarios happen far too often—to the point where I run down store aisles and hide behind huge toilet-paper displays just to avoid a familiar face whose name I can't recall.

The good news is that our Father knows us by name. *By name!* No matter where life takes us, if we settle on the far side of the sea, His hand will guide us. If we hide out in some podunk town, He is there. And get this. He has the hairs on our head numbered—whether we're going through chemo or not! We never have to worry that He will forget us. He knows every intimate detail about us. We are His! ✳ *Diann*

Today's Prayer

Father, thank You for knowing me so intimately. I never need wonder if You know me by name. Your Word says You do, and that's enough. May my name be a sweet incense before You.

I Wanna Hold Your Hand

Trust in the LORD with all your heart
and lean not on your own understanding.

PROVERBS 3:5

For the past several days, I've been pondering this verse. I thought about how many worldly things we trust—family, friends, jobs, money, homes, cars, newspapers, magazines, and even hobbies. As Christians, we want to live our lives close to people and things we can trust. But no matter how wonderful that sounds, all those things will let us down—even family and friends. The only thing we can count on is the Lord. Yesterday, that point was driven home...or should I say *pounded* home?

My husband wanted to play golf, so I decided to go visit my dad and step-mom. Her birthday was coming up soon, so it seemed like a good time to bring her a gift and spend a little time with them, not having seen them in a while. I'd been there a couple of hours when my cell phone rang. The caller ID said HOME, so I knew it was my husband. I assumed he was asking where I was, when I planned to return home, and what was for dinner.

Instead, he said something that made my heart drop. "I was injured on the golf course," he stated, his voice all gravely. "As I turned the corner in the golf cart, my foot hit a curb, and something in my ankle snapped. What should I do?"

After asking if he thought it was broken and getting his I-don't-know reply, I paused for a moment to think about how long it would take me to get home and bring him to the emergency room. An hour—too long. So I asked him if he could drive himself to the hospital. I felt terrible, like I was letting him down. If I'd been home, he could have leaned on me and we would have immediately been on our way to get medical attention.

He assured me he could drive, so I hung up, said my good-byes to my dad and step-mom, then hurried home. An hour later, Wally hobbled into the house, leaning on crutches. "These things are hard to maneuver," he said. Once he placed them against the wall, he didn't pick them up again. Instead, he hopped around.

Proverbs 3:5 popped into my head. Although the verse isn't talking about physical crutches, it's easy to compare them to our understanding and how different that is from the Lord's strength. Crutches are annoying and cumbersome, while the Lord's strong shoulders are always there for us to rely on. ✳ *Debby*

Today's Prayer

Lord, heavenly Father, I pray that I will stop placing
all my trust in worldly things and lean more on You. The strength
You provide is so much more than anything family, friends,
or even physical crutches can offer. Take my hand, Lord,
and lead me to do Your will. Amen.

From Dust Bunny to Dust

As a father has compassion on his children,
so the LORD has compassion on those who fear him.

PSALM 103:13

Not everyone dusts the house the way I do. Many people dust more often than once a presidential term. I always mean to do better, but the truth is, if I didn't host my book club meetings a few times a year, we'd be talking scenes from *Tales from the Crypt* around here. The house is *clean*, but it does get dusty.

Part of the problem is that, no matter how hard I try, that doggone dust comes right back again. Despite the sweat of my brow, there is simply no way to ban the dust long-term. So I kind of gave up awhile ago.

I'm thankful God isn't like me. No matter how often I come back—feeble, sinful, selfish, and disobedient—He doesn't give up on me. He doesn't give up on any of us. The next verse provides a hint as to why God is so patient with us. "As a father has compassion on his children, so the LORD has compassion on those who fear him; *for he knows how we are formed, he remembers that we are dust*" (Psalm 103:13–14).

Even *I* couldn't gather up enough dust to form an entire human. But the Lord has the wherewithal and the power to do exactly that. When we fail, God never forgets the fact that—although He loves us unconditionally—we are but dust. I ask you, fellow dust bunny: how do we merit that kind of love?

Sometimes we don't even *try* to deserve His love. Sometimes we get all puffed up about ourselves and our rights, our pride, our expectations of respect and consideration. God doesn't forget our origins, but sometimes we do.

And how about when we *do* try to deserve His love? No matter how hard we might try, there is no way for us to get it right. No way to become innocent children of God. No way to achieve the right to call ourselves His. No way except *One*.

God knew when He formed us from the dust that we'd fall short. Jesus knew it too. And the Holy Spirit has always been ready, just waiting for us to receive God's gift, to ask Jesus to forgive and save us, and to accept the filling of the Holy Spirit.

One of the kindest considerations our Father gives us is His constant compassion. Yes, we are to "fear" our Father by respecting Him, but we need never fear He will brush "the dust" off His sandals and reject us, even though we keep coming back dirty and imperfect.

God isn't like I am with dust, disgusted when it shows up again. He *loves* that we keep coming back. ✳ Trish

Today's Prayer

Lord, thank You for forming me. Thank You for forgiving me.
Thank You for loving me, over and over again. Amen.

The Gift of Trey

*"Ask and it will be given to you; seek and you will find;
knock and the door will be opened to you."*

MATTHEW 7:7

Help! Please!"

I've heard it said that those are the only purely honest prayers.
I don't know if that's true or not, but I know I've had my fair share of
"Help!" and "Please" prayers when I felt too weak or too overwhelmed to
pray, because the pain of not having that prayer answered seemed unfathomable to me.

When I was pregnant with my first child, something felt *wrong*. I went
to the doctor, and at eleven weeks, the doctor coldly stated, "Nothing. No
baby." My heart sank.

No, not my baby, God, please!

To make matters worse, a family member had impregnated his girlfriend and the baby was due the same day. I had to endure the baby showers, the wedding, and watching her blossom with child, all for someone
who did it "wrong"—while not knowing if I would ever be a mother.

Sure, it was selfish. When we're hurting, we're not exactly beacons
of sainthood. Sometimes we're more like spoiled children, stamping our
feet for what we want *and want now!*

I had to work through those feelings and appreciate my relation's
gift, while mourning my own loss and knowing that God's will is perfect,
even if it felt unfair, irrational, and highlighted by someone else's good
fortune. But God wants the best for us, and sometimes we have to trust
that He knows what it is.

That doesn't stop us from desperate prayers, of course. We're only
human. If I hadn't lost that first baby, I might not have had my Trey,
who is the greatest firstborn any mother could dream of. Maybe his three

fantastic siblings would be different; who knows? All I know is that painful experience brought me the greatest day of my life: *Trey's birth.*

Looking back, hindsight is 20/20, and God knew what He was doing. I try to remember that in present circumstances when His will seems to conflict with my own, but I don't always succeed. Let's face it. *I want what I want when I want it.* Don't we all, if we're honest? But we have to remember to ask, and if we're too weak to ask, that's when a glorious Friend can intervene for us.

Hebrews 11:1 tells us that faith is the substance of things hoped for, the evidence of things not seen (KJV). Sometimes I do wish it would be more obvious, but that's why I have to look back and remember. ✳ *Kristin*

Today's Prayer

Dear Jesus, thank You for showing me that
Your way is always best. Help me to remember Your great
love for me and my life when I am feeling neglected
and lonely. Help me to ask, however weak my pleading
may be. You know the desires of my heart. Amen.

My Life as a Piñata

Hope deferred makes the heart sick, but a longing fulfilled is a tree of life.

PROVERBS 13:12

The Colleen Cobles and Jasmine Cresswells of the world have a gift for writing suspense. Oh, how I admire that ability. The Andrea Boeshaars and Nicholas Sparkses can grab hold of a reader's heartstrings, and they just don't let go. It seems like all of the great ones have a specific calling on their writing, a certain branding that defines them as writers.

When a new line of romantic comedy was announced, I excitedly approached the editor and gave her my pitch. She read the first couple of pages of what I had in mind and seemed almost enthusiastic when she asked me to put together a full proposal. I agonized over it for weeks before sending her a synopsis and three chapters. Then I waited.

Instead of a form letter, I received a phone call from the editor several months later. Hope inflated my heart as I waited to hear the words I felt certain she planned to utter: "Congratulations! I'd like to offer you..."

Talk about hope deferred! What I heard instead began with, "Look. I can see that you *think* you're really funny. But I'm here to tell you, Sandie, you are *not*."

The poor little corpse of my hope thudded to the pit of my stomach. I was heartbroken—and I felt physically ill as she went on for nearly fifteen minutes, telling me why I would likely never have a career as an author, most assuredly not writing romantic comedy, and certainly not for her publishing house.

It took me awhile to recover from that, but I somehow managed to dig through the rubble and find my calling again. For five years, I honed my craft and continued to write in spite of that editor's song playing in the back of my mind.

You know how the Scriptures often say that God "suddenly" turns circumstances? Like in Acts 2:2, as the apostles awaited the return of the Lord and "*suddenly* a sound like the blowing of a violent wind came from heaven." One day the editor of a new line of inspirational romance contacted me about writing something for them. On that very day, a small bud emerged from the depths of my long-deferred hope. With the launch of *Love Finds You in Snowball, Arkansas*, I became known as an author of "Laugh-Out-Loud" romantic fiction. Six more comedies have followed, awards have been won, mail from readers has confirmed the call on my life, and my subsequent "tree of life" is flourishing beyond what I ever imagined.

Isn't that *so like Him*? Beauty for ashes, my friends; that's just how our God rolls. ✳ Sandie

Today's Prayer

Lord, I am so grateful and humbled to know that this
one little life has Your stamp upon it. Help me to remember
every day, no matter what the obstacles, that I am here to
serve You. And in doing so, I will one day see my deferred
hope fade into a blossoming tree of life. Amen.

Unfinished Business

The Lord will fulfill his purpose for me; your love, O Lord,
endures forever—do not abandon the works of your hands.

PSALM 138:8

In my younger days as a stay-at-home mom, I had plenty to do but still looked for more to keep busy. After all, as my mother would say, "Idle hands are the devil's workshop."

It was years before I realized that wasn't in the Bible.

So with plenty of ambition, I learned how to do cross-stitch, make baskets and pinecone wreaths, sew, knit, crochet, and quilt. One would think that by the age of fifty-four I would have mastered at least a number of these ambitions, but instead all I have to show for it are boxes of incomplete projects. Yes, that's right. I said "incomplete projects." There's my nasty little secret laid bare before you.

It most likely shocks you to the core. It certainly did my husband. Always one to finish what he's started, I'm sure he had no idea when we were dating, sipping soda from the same cup and staring into each another's starry eyes, that he was falling in love with a woman who left partial cross-stitch quotes and buckets of aging pinecones lying around, untouched basket reeds still bunched together, faded fabrics lining the shelves, and colored yarns not yet rolled into balls.

Oh, the shame of it all.

To illustrate our differences further, my husband has a beautiful tenor voice. When in college, if the melodious strains of an aria had drifted through an open dorm window with all but the final note and my husband had been passing by, there is no doubt in my mind that he would have moved heaven and earth to search for a piano to play that last chord. He's a finisher, pure and simple.

When my husband drags me to the shed and points to the bowing shelves crowded with boxes of cottons, polyesters, basket reeds, handles, knitting needles, crochet needles, pinecones, cross-stitch threads, and quilting hoops, all worked in different stages of completion, I tell him I'm waiting for inspiration to strike. The look in his eye says he wouldn't mind giving me a whack of inspiration.

I don't know why he gets so worked up about it. I've no doubt I'll get back to them...one of these days. In the meantime, I have to admit, I'm encouraged to know that God doesn't abandon the works of His hands. He finishes what He starts. Of course, He's dealing with people and I'm dealing with man-made materials. Still, I suppose I should do something about my unfinished projects.

That settles it. Tomorrow I'll take the boxes to Goodwill. Besides, my daughter just called. She wants to teach me how to scrapbook.... ✸ *Diann*

Today's Prayer

I'm so thankful that You never give up on us, Father.
Though I am a work-in-progress, You will be faithful
to complete the good work You have started in me. Amen.

Hey, Baby, What's Your Sign?

For no one can lay any foundation other
than the one already laid, which is Jesus Christ.

1 CORINTHIANS 3:11

$\mathcal{S}$how me a woman who started dating in the sixties, seventies, or eighties, and I'll show you a woman who has heard, "Hey, baby, what's your sign?" at least once. And if she didn't marry the first guy she dated, I'm sure she heard it many more times. That question is good for a laugh and makes a good icebreaker though, right?

Not so much. When a guy asks for your sign, he's talking about your astrological sign. Where's the harm in that? Well, any time we look at something that even attempts to compete with our faith in Christ, we're playing in dangerous territory. It may seem innocent, but anything to do with astrology is based on false teachings, and God condemns it. In Jeremiah 10:2, the Lord says, " 'Do not learn the ways of the nations or be terrified by signs in the sky, though the nations are terrified by them.' " I think this is pretty clear that we're not to look at the stars and planets for signs that predict our future.

I have to admit that I used to read my horoscope in the newspaper first thing in the morning. I never really took it seriously, and it seemed like a fun thing to do. It gave me something to talk about when I got to work, and everyone compared notes to see how our "stars lined up" with each other. If something went wrong during the day, we'd laugh, shrug it off, and blame our astrological sign. It was all done in good fun. Now that I know better, I look back and cringe. Astrology separates us from God by claiming that the stars and planets have more control over us than our Creator. That is just wrong. I strongly believe that only God knew my future when I was born—not some impersonal planet that doesn't have the ability to care or save me from my sin.

When we go through difficult times—which seem to be in abundance lately—it's tempting to reach out for the first thing that offers hope. But the hope isn't in our horoscope in the daily newspaper or someone claiming to know you based on your sun and moon sign. The only place where we can find solace and eternal peace is in God's Word. No matter how much fun it is or how many people around me bring it up, I've learned to just shake my head and say, "No, thank you. I already know my eternal future." ✳ *Debby*

Today's Prayer

Thank You, Lord Jesus, for giving me the promise
of something much more powerful than the stars and planets
to determine who I am and where I'm going. May my eyes
always be focused on You and Your promises. Amen.

Choices

This day I call heaven and earth as witnesses against you that I have set
before you life and death, blessings and curses. Now choose life, so that you
and your children may live and that you may love the LORD your God,
listen to his voice, and hold fast to him. For the LORD is your life.

DEUTERONOMY 30:19–20

Most adult women—like me—can't remember any great stretch of time when they haven't been on some kind of diet. My teen years were diet-free, but, mercy, that was some other gal—that size-four wonder who hadn't a clue how fortunate she was, with her ignorance of consequences yet to come.

In my whippersnapper years, I ate whatever I wanted and suffered absolutely no affects. Today I *smell* a chocolate éclair and not only do I gain weight, but something somewhere gets squishier. So now I weigh the consequences of my culinary choices more than I did in my carefree youth.

As a matter of fact, today I weigh the consequences of *all* my choices more readily than I did when I was younger. The Lord surely did look after this fine young idiot. Each day He set before me life and death, blessings and curses, and left choices open to me. So often I chose poorly. He must have shaken His head and said, "Okay, let's try this again tomorrow. I'll give you another chance."

Perhaps years from now I'll look back on today and say the same thing: "Wow, I had no clue how poorly I chose on a day-to-day basis. And I thought I was doing so well!" The Lord seems to accept that I'm doing the best I can, that I want very much to make decisions that will not only be good for me—for my health, my long-term goals, my children, my sphere of influence—but will also fit within His will for me. How can I do better?

We need to consider that even God's patience can be taxed. As He told Moses in Deuteronomy, He tells us: "*This day*...I have set before you life and death, blessings and curses. Now choose life." He expects us to be active in how we live our lives and how we choose.

How do we know if we are truly "choosing life," as he advised Moses to do? We need look only a few words further in Deuteronomy to get a clue. "Now choose life, so that you and your children may live and that you may love the LORD your God, *listen to his voice, and hold fast to him. For the LORD is your life.*"

For the Lord is your life. That's what we're to choose, daily: the Lord. Listen. Hold fast. *He* is your life. ✳ *Trish*

Today's Prayer

Lord, yesterday I chose You. Today I choose You. Tomorrow, if You'll give me yet another chance, I'll choose You. Help me to remember how important it is—to me and to my children—that I start each day proclaiming, "I choose You." Amen.

Control Freak

Our God is a God who saves; from the
Sovereign LORD comes escape from death.
PSALM 68:20

Jused to be afraid to fly. I'm convinced that it was about the lack of control. Handing my safety over to a complete stranger behind the door is as irrational to me as giving my power to the Wizard of Oz—the man behind the curtain, if you will. So if I did travel, it was done with clutched fingers around the armrests and lots of prayer.

Then, one day after 9/11, I got a call to go on a television show in New York to talk about my book. The only thing I'd rather do *less* than talk publicly about my book is to do so on the other side of the country in New York City with only a day's notice.

It was the day of my son's eighth birthday party, and everything went wrong that day. I didn't have time to get a new outfit for TV; I didn't have time to stop for cash; and I wasn't that great at traveling, so I didn't know that taxis in NYC don't take credit cards. Once on the ground, I also got word that the publicist changed hotels on me and my directions were no longer valid.

In other words, everything that could go wrong—did.

But you know what? God had all of it covered. For instance, the hotel was high-end, and the bellman paid my cab fare until I could get cash.

That trip changed my life. No, I didn't do all that well on TV, and I did miss my son's birthday party, and I was also the coldest I have ever been in my life because of my inability to understand what real winter feels like. But I learned something that day.

I learned that God is truly in control and that if I believe it, I have nothing to fear. If it's my day to go, He's got that covered too because all I have to do is believe on the Lord Jesus Christ, confess that belief with my mouth, and I will be saved from eternal death.

When we spend our time worrying, we are spending our time saying that God isn't there, that He can't handle this one thing...and that's just not true. My will may not be His, but His is better.

Now I fly at least once a month. Travel is no longer a fear, and I enjoy every moment of my trips. That was worth everything not going my way, right? ✳ *Kristin*

Today's Prayer

Dear Jesus, thank You for reminding me that
You are in control and that no matter what I do,
nothing can separate me from Your love. May I work
today to put worries aside and put my trust in You. Amen.

Just Do It

We live by faith, not by sight.
2 Corinthians 5:7

I was twenty-five years old when I turned a corner and suddenly the life I'd come to know was gone. No more marriage, home, job, or familiarity with anyone or anything. With nothing more than what I could fit into the back of a Ford Fiesta, I drove for two days to start my life over. And for a girl who'd grown up in Cincinnati, Ohio, I felt like a dot on the map in a city as vast as Los Angeles.

I moved in with the family of someone I'd met when I was a teenager; we'd been little more than pen pals over the years in between. But for some reason I never fully understood, she and her mother opened their home to this wayward mess of a person and gave me a roof over my head until I could figure it all out.

The job search turned very bleak very fast, and one afternoon just two weeks after my arrival in Southern California, reality took a nosedive with my spirits strapped onboard. "The only experience I have is office work," I told my friend. "And the thought of being a secretary for the rest of my life is almost unbearable."

Roanne sighed in reply. "Well," she said, "what would be your dream job? If you could do anything you wanted to do, what would it be?" I laughed. "I would be a writer." "What kind of writer?" "Any kind. Ideally, a screenwriter or a novelist. But since that's not likely to happen…"

After a moment's thought, Roanne left the room. When she returned a few minutes later, she dragged a huge manual typewriter to the counter, piled a stack of blank white paper next to it, and pulled out the bar stool.

"You want to write?" she asked me. Before I could reply, she pointed at the counter. "Forget what you can't do and think about what you can. Write something."

Even now as I retell the story, it sounds ridiculous. But over the next couple of months, in between interviews and temporary office assignments, I tapped out the worst book that's ever been written, and Roanne had the audacity to send it to several publishers. The rejections poured in, and I eventually threw away the typed pages. I wrote three more terrible novels while going to film school at night...and four screenplays after that before one of my scripts was finally optioned.

In that one ridiculous moment, floundering around in the most hopeless and terrifying season of my life, someone looked me in the eyes and told me that my dreams might actually be attainable. And the profound exhilaration that followed rolled out a vision that pushed me forward toward the writer that I am today. ✳ *Sandie*

Today's Prayer

Lord, thank You for showing me early on
what it truly means to believe. Amen.

Morning Wake-Up Call

The Sovereign LORD has given me an instructed tongue,
to know the word that sustains the weary. He wakens me morning
by morning, wakens my ear to listen like one being taught.

ISAIAH 50:4

Morning people amaze me. You know the type. They wake up with smiles on their faces. Then they bounce their way to the kitchen, where they prepare a healthy concoction of fruits, juices, wheat germ, and maybe something that came from the backyard garden.

When I was a kid, I thought those people drove themselves to get up in the morning, and certainly there are those who do (but they are not "morning people" in the truest sense of the word). Imagine my horror when I discovered that there were people who actually—wait for it—love to get up with the rising of the morning sun!

This is just wrong on so many levels.

I wish I could tell you that when the alarm goes off, I automatically spring into action. But honestly, nary a muscle moves on my body until the alarm screams at least three times, and then only the slightest twitch of a nerve gives a faint indication of life inside this physical shell. If not for the scent of coffee luring my pajama-clad, fluffy-slippered self into the kitchen, I'd probably stay in bed till noon.

Now, make no mistake, I do not get up with the rising of the sun. I've heard it's a beautiful sight, but I witness sunrise enough on the front of my Raisin Bran box. I want to sleep as late as possible. It's truly better for everyone in my world.

Still, we all know that duty calls. There is work to be done, calls to be made, lists to be accomplished. So I drag myself out of bed and reluctantly give in to the start of a new day.

Before I dive into my workday, however, I open God's Word and see what He wants to tell me, and then we "discuss" it. It's during my morning prayer that He will bring to mind those for whom I need to pray, call, visit, or send a card. I love when He plans my day. How rewarding it is when someone says they received the card or phone call just when they needed it. Of course, it was because God knew their need and prompted me to help His work.

I don't look forward to mornings, but I do look forward to my time with Him. It's in my quiet place that I find His perspective, guidance, grace, mercy, joy, and strength for another day.

We are His hands and feet. He wants to use us in our world to make a difference for the kingdom—whether it's morning, noon, or evening. Are you listening? ✳ *Diann*

Today's Prayer

Father, I yield my wants and plans for this day
to Your leading. Use me as You will to offer
encouragement to the weary.

Too Much
of a Good Thing

It is not good to eat too much honey,
nor is it honorable to seek one's own honor.

PROVERBS 25:27

After I grew tired of scrimping and pinching pennies, I got a part-time job as a merchandising sales representative for a candy company about twenty years ago. My boss sent me home with a huge stash of candy at the end of my first day of training. Until then, my kids rarely had sugar—mostly only for special occasions. I walked through the door and placed it on the kitchen counter without a second thought before going upstairs to do some chores while my kids watched a movie.

When I came back down, my older daughter, Alison, who was seven or eight at the time, lay on the couch clutching her stomach. "I ate too much Laffy Taffy," she moaned. I went into the kitchen and glanced at the counter. At least a third of the candy was missing.

I looked over at my other daughter, Lauren, who smiled and said, "I'm not sick. I didn't eat too much." That was a relief, because having one sick little girl was enough.

Although Proverbs 25:27 isn't speaking directly to eating too much Laffy Taffy, it does relate in a symbolic sort of way. A little bit of a good thing is...well, good. Too much can be nauseating and take our focus away from God. It can also create an extreme dislike of whatever was overdone. To this day, I bet Alison would be perfectly happy if she never saw another piece of purple Laffy Taffy again. Even the reminder of that day twenty years ago elicits a groan.

In this world of overindulgence, it's easy to overdo anything—from food and personal possessions to ambition. A little bit of career ambition is fine because it generally brings an income for the family and respect from peers. However, too much often leads to greed and contempt. Climbing the corporate ladder has provided many people with fat wallets and empty lives. Then there's athletic ambition. We've all heard of those overachievers who are determined to win at all costs and willing to abuse their bodies, their friends, and their spiritual lives to have that moment of glory. But once they step down off that pedestal, it's over. What then?

As a Christian, I'm working hard at not wanting more of what I already have. It's so easy to fall into the trap of craving "one more" of anything because one more leads to another, and it never seems to stop until it harms us. Scripture is very clear that the only thing we can't get too much of is time with Him in His word. ✳ *Debby*

Today's Prayer

Dear Lord, may I learn to be satisfied with enough
and not long for more than I need. The wisdom in Your Word
shows time and again that this is the way we should live. Amen.

Jacob's God

May the LORD answer you when you are in distress;
may the name of the God of Jacob protect you.

PSALM 20:1

Most of us remember life before cell phones. Travel back in time with me, children, *way* back to the days of disco. I was young, single, living paycheck-to-paycheck, and enjoying life. After a long night of dancing the bump and the hustle, I was headed home when my car broke down.

To this day, I notice how dark some roads would be at night if it weren't for our headlights. I do that because of the night in question. My car died on an unlit road with no traffic. I became frighteningly aware of how stranded I was. I was an hour's walk from my apartment, dressed in a sparkly disco minidress and heels, surrounded on either side by black, dense woods. And to make matters especially bad, there had been a number of assaults on local women that month.

Distressed? You betcha. These days, a damsel in distress would whip out her cell phone and summon help right away. I didn't have time to wait for the invention of the cell phone. I turned immediately to God. I wasn't yet a Christian, but I believed in God...and it didn't take brilliance to understand I wasn't going to get help anywhere else. I was terrified and crying, but I started walking home and prayed out loud all the while.

A carload of young men pulled up beside me, and they offered me a ride home. None of them looked like they could be Jack the Ripper, but I was savvy enough not to take comfort in that. Still, I didn't know what else to do. I was willing to walk all the way home; I just didn't know if I'd make it before falling prey to someone dangerous. And I didn't know if that someone dangerous was sitting right there in that car.

Are you thinking these men were God's answer to my prayers? Nope. That answer came when yet another car pulled up behind the first.

Despite the late hour and the fact that I knew few people in town, the couple who lived right next door to me were in the second car. They didn't recognize me until they felt led to pull over. Even they were amazed by the "coincidence" and curious about how matters might have evolved had they not happened down the road when they did.

The God of Jacob... You know, Jacob wasn't exactly the poster boy for the fine, upstanding Christian believer. Yet God protected him the way He protected me that night. May the Lord answer your prayers of distress in the same way. ✱ Trish

Today's Prayer

Lord, I know my distress might not equal that of others, and neither may my faith. But I pray You will protect me when I call out to You. I won't get Your kind of help anywhere else. Amen.

Cheap Runs Deep

Give portions to seven, yes to eight, for you do not know
what disaster may come upon the land.

ECCLESIASTES 11:2

There are few things in life that can ruin one's witness as a Christian faster than being cheap. Some call it *frugal*, but think about it. You had a friend, somewhere in your history—you know the one—where you all planned to put in an extra couple of bucks because her "portion" wouldn't cover the tax and tip in a restaurant. And it wasn't because she couldn't afford it. *That* friend.

I grew up with a very generous family, but neither my grandparents nor my parents possessed a lot of money when I was a child. One of the biggest "outings" in our family was when my cousins and I went to see my grandfather's bridge in Menlo Park, California. Grandpa had made a bridge with curved wood at the local civic center. He'd tell us about all the engineering and work that went into building a "curve" into wood, and we'd listen patiently because he'd take us to Foster's Freeze for ice cream cones once we were done. Kids will endure a lot for ice cream.

Although I can't ever remember him spending more than twenty dollars on me at any time, Grandpa would treat me to lunch at Burger King when I was in high school. The most expensive thing I recall is a dress he bought me at J.C. Penney's for kindergarten. We fought over the color.

My grandfather is 94 now, living in the lap of luxury at a gorgeous retirement home, where his biggest trouble is trying to get the coveted seat in the sunshine after lunchtime...or if he doesn't like the soup of the day. His money lasted because he saved; he scrimped, but he was never cheap. And if my grandfather ever did run out of money before he ran out of life, there would be countless loved ones there to rescue him from his fate...because he invested in what really mattered.

When I think of today's verse, I think of my grandpa and grandma: always careful, always aware of the future, never cheap. When you invest your money, are you thoughtful of where it goes? Do you deny yourself rather than someone else? Is someone else's tip a place where you find savings? If so, think of God's promise to care for you and what true value means. ✳ *Kristin*

Today's Prayer

Dear heavenly Father, You have preordained the money
I would have in this lifetime. Help me to be a strong steward of it,
to use it in love and always to find value in where I am today.

First Things First

Finish your outdoor work and get your fields ready;
after that, build your house.

PROVERBS 24:27

I've been dreaming of owning my own home for a very long time. I came close when I was living in California, but when I made the move to Florida and started over, it looked like a faraway dream that might never come to fruition.

I muddled through a disheartening season where it seemed like everyone I knew went house-hunting and ended up buying something. I made offers on three different homes and someone beat me to the punch every time. It bordered on the ridiculous when a longtime friend phoned to tell me that her brother had purchased a home *for her*.

Finding a home of my own finally wrangled my full focus: I researched the best mortgage brokers; talked to Realtors; looked into lenders and loans for first-time buyers; Googled neighborhoods within a fifteen-mile radius and explored them thoroughly.

During that period, I also sold a couple more books and accepted a promotion at my day job. The added income lined my fledgling savings account, earmarked "Future Home." Meanwhile, I became so tired of the whole "future" concept that some nights I would cry while praying and ask the Lord why it was taking so long to have what every other adult in America seemed to have acquired long ago.

And then one day I found it: a sunny little yellow house in a great neighborhood just a few minutes from my office. When I phoned my Realtor, I learned that the homeowners were facing personal issues and wanted to move as soon as possible. The broker found me a fantastic loan where I wouldn't have to put down any money at all; in fact, at closing, I came away with a check! The movers charged me less than they quoted.

I came across a handyman so reasonable and fair that a move-in-ready home welcomed me within a week of closing. And the icing on the cake? I slid in under the velvet rope with eligibility for the federal tax credit for first-time buyers just a couple of weeks before the offer expired.

I'm often asked if I'm sorry I had to wait such a long time. My reply: "Are you joking?"

In the spirit of the Scripture that says to prepare your life first and then build your home, I am confident, humbled, and thankful. When I walk through my house early in the morning or sit and look out the window just before sunset, I am inspired *every time* to thank the Lord for holding up the works. My heart's desire rolled out before me like a choreographed production with a very happy ending. ✳ *Sandie*

Today's Prayer

Praise You, Lord Jesus, for Your amazing ability
to plan ahead. I'm in awe! Help me to remember every day
that You have it all mapped out for me. Amen.

Hairless Wonder

O LORD, you have searched me and you know me. You know when I sit and when I rise; you perceive my thoughts from afar. You discern my going out and my lying down; you are familiar with all my ways.

PSALM 139:1–3

Once I learned that I needed chemo, I decided to take action and get my head shaved ahead of time. If I was going to look like Bruce Willis, *I* would make it happen, not the chemo. I was determined to wear stylish turbans and wigs of all colors and lengths, which would, no doubt, cast suspicion upon my sweet, faithful husband who would be seen with a "different" woman every night.

So while I was at the Cancer Treatment Center of America, I made arrangements to go to the salon and have my hair cut. The stylist had done this many times for patients, so I felt secure in her capable hands.

In the back room, away from prying eyes, she talked to me about what she would do before she set to work. I was fine—until the buzz of the clippers jarred my raw nerves. I saw a strand of long hair fall to the floor. The air suddenly turned thick, and it was hard to breathe. My chest grew tight. I wanted to scream at the injustice of it all, to say the cancer, the appointment, everything was a mistake. This couldn't be happening to me.

Oh, God, where are you? I can't do this!

Then, amazingly, God's Word flooded my heart: "O Lord, you have searched me and you know me." *Falling hair. So much hair.* "You know when I sit and when I rise." *Do you see what she's doing to me? Make her stop!* "You perceive my thoughts from afar." *I'm so scared.* "You discern my going out and my lying down; you are familiar with all my ways."

Naked. Exposed. Vulnerable. Frail.

"Lean on Me. We'll get through this...together."

That day, I sensed His tears mingle with mine and fall to the floor with my hair. His words melted over me and calmed my spirit in a way my words can never adequately explain. From that moment on, I knew I would get through this, one step at a time, come what may, because He would never leave me.

I don't know what you're facing, but if He can calm me in the midst of my storm, He can do it for you—and He will do it for you, if you ask Him. Our Father who knows us better than anyone and loves us infinitely more than we could ever imagine is here for You. Will you go to Him with your need? He's waiting. ✳ *Diann*

Today's Prayer

Merciful and gracious God, no one knows me and loves me the way You do. Help that truth to permeate every fiber of my being, that I may trust You more...come what may. Amen.

Show Me the Money

The LORD sends poverty and wealth; he humbles and he exalts.

1 SAMUEL 2:7

My husband has been in the financial-services industry for many years. We've seen both ends of the poverty/wealth spectrum in many of his clients. There isn't a big difference in people's expectations between those with the highest and the lowest net worths. The most significant distinguishing factor seems to be their faith that ties in with their view of life, regardless of how much money is in their account.

I know from our personal experiences of struggling while my husband built his business that not having money is frustrating, but our faith kept us together as a family; we never doubted God's love because He never abandoned us at any time. He made sure we had a roof over our heads, something to wear, and food on the table. After my husband's business matured, we knew God still had our backs and loved us the same as always. That never changed, even when our circumstances did. We actually became comfortable, and we were able to do a few things we'd always wanted to do.

Then a couple of years ago, the economy tanked and there was no longer quite as much money coming in because my husband, kindhearted man that he is, spent countless hours working for his clients to salvage as much as he could of their hard-earned money without regard for his own income. Fortunately, our daughters were already grown and self-supporting, so our current income needs aren't as great as they once were.

The Lord's will in our lives is based on what He knows we need at the time. He uses both poverty and wealth to teach us, love us, and discipline us in ways we may not understand. As difficult as it has been at times, accepting the fluctuations in income has become almost second nature to my husband and me. Occasionally He needs to bring us to our knees, and He does it so effectively.

Money is mentioned in the Bible hundreds of times, so God obviously considers it relevant to our lives. His perspective is quite different from ours, though, and I think we need to pay closer attention to what He says. He's not so much against having wealth, but He warns us about our attitude toward it. I've found that when I looked at money to define anything about myself as a person, I've been miserable, regardless of how much I had or didn't have. On the flip side, when my focus is on Him, I see money as something that comes when needed and goes when it becomes too consuming, and I find joy in His promise of eternal life. ✱ Debby

Today's Prayer

Thank You, oh Lord, for blessing us with what we need.
You have never failed to provide for us. Please continue
guarding us from the temptations of the evil one and
guiding us with Your discipline and love. Amen.

When We Forget Who's Listening

Those who look to him are radiant;
their faces are never covered with shame.

PSALM 34:5

Years ago, when my son was in grade school, he and a couple of his friends from church were playing just below my open bedroom window—so I happened to hear when the two friends decided to teach my son how to spell a vulgar word in sign language. They actually said each of the letters as they formed them, so the irony of their getting busted while using sign language was not lost on me. They were sweet, well-behaved kids; their play had simply degenerated gradually without their noticing it.

To his credit, my son didn't join in the high jinks, but I calmly went downstairs and called him in along with the other boys. The other boys' moms were (and are) dear friends of mine, and I knew they would prefer I didn't ignore this "teaching moment."

I brought the boys back to my room and could tell they were completely unaware that I had heard them. But the window was still open. I had them stand near the window, and I simply said, "What can you hear from here?" Birds tweeted clearly. Katydids sang in the trees. The sprinkler ticked back and forth.

It didn't take long for their guilty consciences to fill in the blanks. The melodrama was swift. One of the boys groaned and sank against the wall until he crumpled to the floor and covered his face with his hands. The other burst into tears of shame and fear. My guess is that my son was thanking heaven he had kept his mouth shut.

I still remember being disgraced horribly when, as a child, I behaved in a vulgar manner and got caught by my mother...so I made a point of talking kindly with the boys. I told them they just had to remember that even if another person couldn't hear them, they still needed to try to honor God with their words. I told them adults needed to do that too. But I think they were just relieved I wasn't going to put them in shackles and cart them home to their parents.

Shame is a horrible feeling, and I know I've never done or said anything to merit it without having momentarily forgotten about God first. When I'm in church, wholly focused on worship music, a good sermon, and the Lord's love and guidance, that's probably the closest I'll ever get to radiance, because I'm looking to Him. There's certainly something to be said for surrounding yourself with godly people, godly pleasures, godly teaching, and just...God. ✳ Trish

Today's Prayer

Dearest Lord, if I ever get too far from You and too
caught up in myself and the world, please forgive me
and draw me back to You. Remind me of the radiance
in the faces of those who look to You. Amen.

Entertaining the Angels among Us

Do not forget to entertain strangers, for by so doing some people have entertained angels without knowing it.

HEBREWS 13:2

I grew up with a mentally retarded brother—or "developmentally disabled," as they call it today. In one way, this was a complete gift to me because I got to discover the true insides of a person by how they treated my brother. I've seen educated, wealthy people treat him as though he were something on the bottom of their shoe. And I've seen scary, chain-wearing, leather-clad bikers treat him with their full attention, as if nothing was more important than to hear what he had to say.

When I was in college, I worked in an upscale hotel, and I saw wealthy, spoiled-rotten people treat hotel workers like vermin. There was no gratitude in them. To this day, it breaks my heart that people can treat others this way because of worldly attributes like money, position, or appearance. It's the polar opposite of the way God would want it. His teachings tell us that those qualifiers have nothing to do with His love for us or the love He directs us to have toward others.

Sometimes our ministries and duties at church seem to go unnoticed, and we may wonder if we're not squandering God's time or if we're supposed to do something "more important." Maybe we're not really sure of our purpose—but I know without a doubt that God has a plan for our works. How we treat *the least of these* has a huge impact on hearts all around us. I know this because of my brother and a brief encounter with a stranger. I know this because one day, more than twenty-five years ago, a biker dude was nice to my brother in a Round Table Pizza restaurant. I learned a great deal about entertaining angels that day...and about the way God expects us to behave toward the people in the world around us.

So if someone has ever treated you as if you didn't matter, if you're having a day where you don't feel all that important in terms of God's kingdom and His plans, remember that God views you as the apple of His eye, the object of His affections. He clings to your every word, and He looks you in the eyes as if there's not another place He'd rather be. You matter to Him. ✳ *Kristin*

Today's Prayer

Dear Jesus, when I get to feeling sorry for myself
because my hair isn't right or my outfit isn't ironed,
help me to remember the way You see me—as if Hollywood
doesn't have a bigger star than me, nor do Your heavens.
Help me to pass this love on to others today and remind
someone how important and beautiful they are to this world.

It's Not Where
We Are, It's Where
We're Going

*"Because of the oppression of the weak and
the groaning of the needy, I will now arise," says the LORD.
"I will protect them from those who malign them."*

PSALM 12:5

Rosemary called me last summer to ask if I might be available for a chat. "I don't know what to do," she told me later that day over lattes. "I'm at the end of my rope. I really felt God's leading last year, urging me to get out of debt. The strides I made in the beginning were small, but at least I was progressing toward the goal. This year, it seems like every time I take a step forward, something happens and I'm shoved two steps back."

Isn't that the way? We get a clear picture of the destination, but it seems like all our good intentions are squashed as we make the journey.

It occurs to me, what if I was one of those enemy spirits assigned to trip up the efforts of God's people? I wouldn't just stand at the finish line, waiting for one big battle. As in all things in my life, I would make a game plan. I'd look at the big picture and fill in the gaps with strategies and obstacles to stop the progression. In my friend's case, for instance, I would start early and strike often: a medical bill here, a car problem there, until I finally squandered whatever funds I could get my hands on, setting her back from her ultimate goal.

The good news is that there seems to be a supernatural sort of grace that occurs in those times, and we find the ability to stand up, dust off the frustration and disappointment, and simply carry on.

Last week, Rosemary told me that she is in the home stretch toward her goal. She grinned as she told me, "I have no delusions about it. Someone may slash all four tires on my car next week, or the hot water heater could inexplicably explode. But you know what? I'm going to keep my eyes fixed on where I'm going, not on where I am. When I need Him, that's when God will rise up and do something extraordinary."

I'm encouraged by my friend's ongoing journey, and I find myself remembering her struggles as I wage my own battles toward goals that often seem unreachable. I can hardly wait to rejoice with her when she reaches that destination. Will it be this year that Rosemary declares her victory? Maybe not. But I'm inclined to believe that she'll reach her goal the same way the rest of us will: one step forward and two steps back this week, three steps forward the next. ✳ *Sandie*

Today's Prayer

Thank You for Your ongoing faithfulness, Lord. Help me to be more like You as I run my own race, my eyes fixed on the destination, knowing that You are faithful to get me there. Amen.

Be on Guard

Above all else, guard your heart, for it is the wellspring of life.

PROVERBS 4:23

A conservative politician recently resigned after admitting to an affair with a staff member. His confession appeared genuine and broken. My heart goes out to him as he works to mend his tattered family.

Now, don't get me wrong. I was very disappointed and upset about the matter, to say the least. We expect more from godly people who are telling others to abstain and take the moral high road and yet fail to do so themselves. It's easy to point fingers and say, "They should have known better." And, of course, they should have.

Still, it happens.

I'm not excusing his behavior. It's wrong, pure and simple. Yet, all week long I've been thinking about what could happen in a person's life to bring them to that place of deceit and self-destruction. After much thought and reflection, I've come to the conclusion that we get so busy with the demands in our lives that sometimes we shut God out. It's easy to do. We skip our quiet time because we're late for work. Then the next day, it happens again. By the end of the week, we don't even miss Him. The next thing we know, it's time for church and we have no idea where we've placed our Bible.

The truth is, we try to face life's struggles and temptations in our own strength, and it just doesn't work. There are some things we just cannot battle on our own. We must connect to our life source, the Vine, our Lord, on a daily basis, for much-needed spiritual nourishment.

The sad confession by Mr. Politician made me take stock of my own life. I dare not take a step into my day without spending time with my Lord to refuel. Not because of legalistic reasons, but because I'm very much aware of my own human inadequacy to face the challenges of life. I desperately need His power within me to do His work in a hurting world. "I can do everything *through him* who gives me strength" (Philippians 4:13). That's the only way I can do anything.

How about you? Is God the top priority in your life? Do you ask for His leading before you begin your day, or do you dare to walk the dusty, uncertain path of life on your own? The only true way to guard your heart is to spend time with Him. Confess your need for Him today, and ask Him to strengthen you as you minister to a dark, broken world. Then go out and make a difference. ✳ *Diann*

Today's Prayer

Father, You are the Ruler of all things. There is nothing too hard for You. How thankful I am that You can handle anything that comes my way. Help me to recognize anew that I need You—every day. Amen.

What's a Friend For?

Greater love has no one than this,
that he lay down his life for his friends.

JOHN 15:13

I need your help. An attorney will be here in about fifteen minutes, and he says we have to have witnesses."

This call came from a tearful neighbor after she found out that her husband had a terminal illness. Although they are in their seventies, they didn't have a will until they felt they needed one, and then suddenly it was urgent. So I went next door to witness the signing of the will. My heart ached as I sat across the table from a man whose health is so bad he probably won't be with us much longer. My hand shook as I wrote my name beneath his, and it took every bit of my self-control to keep from crying. I *so* didn't want to be there, but they needed me.

I've called friends to help me with various things—from asking for advice on an outfit for a special event to moving my furniture when I couldn't afford to hire professionals. Most of those times, my friends were right there, ready and willing to do whatever was needed. And I appreciated every bit of assistance they gave.

My friends were willing to take risks for me by coming when I called. When I asked if an outfit made me look like a wide load from the rear, I expected honesty—but there was no guarantee my feelings wouldn't be hurt. A true friend would tell me and gently steer me to something more flattering, at the risk of upsetting me. One friend offered to come over and watch my children so my husband and I could have a date night. When I asked for help with moving furniture, I was asking my friends to take a day out of their busy lives, sweat in intense Florida heat, and risk injury to themselves when they picked up my triple dresser and king-size bed.

I'm grateful for my friends because they're almost always willing to come through for me. I want to be a friend to others, even when it involves taking risks. But when I think about what God did by sending His Son to die for us...*whoa!* That's way more than we can request from any friend on earth. I can't even imagine asking anyone to give up his or her life for me. The beauty of God's sacrifice is even more amazing since we never had to ask for it. He did it because He knew we needed salvation—something we could never handle on our own. Talk about a true, everlasting friend! He's the friend we should open our hearts to above all others. ✳ *Debby*

Today's Prayer

Thank You, Jesus, for being a best friend to all believers. Lead me to continue opening my heart to You and share the joy of this friendship with others. I will never doubt Your loyalty as I reflect on Your sacrifice. Amen.

Eagle's Wings

But those who hope in the LORD will renew their strength.
They will soar on wings like eagles; they will run and not grow weary,
they will walk and not be faint.

ISAIAH 40:31

One of my favorite parts in *Lord of the Rings* is when Gandalf the wizard is rescued from atop evil Saruman's tower by Gwaihir, a massive eagle. (Note: I had to look up most of those names—I'm not a *total* nerd.) The scene is exhilarating and provides Gandalf (and the viewer) great relief. Before the eagle arrives, the poor man—er, wizard—is completely exhausted after a long, bitter battle; he's stuck in a spot where no one can help him; and goodness knows the last time he had a shower or a decent meal.

Some days I can totally identify. I'll bet you can too. Maybe you have a house to keep, a family to raise, a husband to please, a job to finish, and far too little time in your day. Maybe your situation isn't even *that* good. You can't afford a house, you have strife in your family (or *no* family), you can't *find* a job, and the days slip past you at an alarming rate.

On those days, I wish a massive eagle would swoop down and fly me somewhere far away from my responsibilities and worries. But I'd settle for a cleaning crew, a secretary, a chauffeur, a beauty entourage, and a yacht full of cash. I mean, the chances of my getting all that are as good as the chance that I'm going to be soaring on wings of eagles anytime soon, right?

But God promises that soaring to us, if we hope in Him. Other translations of today's verse address those who *wait* on the Lord and those who *trust* in Him. So God wants us to hope, wait, and trust. That, I think I can do.

When you think about it, that's what our faith is all about. When we give our lives to Jesus and tell Him we believe He's done it all for us—saved us from a horrible spot where no one else could have helped us—we're placing all our hopes in Him. We're agreeing to wait, as long as He dictates, for blissful, perfect eternity (and even for every blessing He has planned for us here on earth). We're saying we trust everything He's said and done, no matter what happens while we live on earth.

Regardless of what you experience in life—soaring happiness or wearying adversity—knowing you've placed it all on His shoulders *does* renew your strength, don't you think? Each time we renew our hope, He'll renew our strength. ✳ *Trish*

Today's Prayer

Lord Jesus, I do hope in You. I trust in You.
And I'll wait as long as You want me to for the blessings
and strength You plan for me. Help me continue
to walk with You and not grow faint. Amen.

Broken Hearts Restored!

A man's spirit sustains him in sickness,
but a crushed spirit who can bear?

PROVERBS 18:14

This is such a profound verse because the human body can endure so much. Once, I interviewed an incredible Christian woman who had been shot more than twenty-six times. A victim of terrorism, she was the only survivor in a car of five missionaries. Her husband, who had battled to get to her safely to the hospital, died from the attack.

What I remember most vividly about the interview—which was less than a year after this tragedy happened—was not her body's wounds, which included a gouge the size of a tennis ball in her knee. I remember her heart. It was broken. She trusted God's plan. She knew the Lord had spared her for a reason, but she woke up across the world in a Texas hospital with her life completely changed. Her husband was with Jesus; her hand was permanently disfigured; and her own hopes of having a child with her husband were forever dashed.

The human body is amazing. God has created it to have restorative, healing powers...but our hearts are different. If you've ever been in a place where hope is absent, where God's reasons are unfathomable, where His voice is silent, you understand. When the body is weak, we can hope for a different future. We might even see peace in the quiet time to pray. But where hope is absent, the heart truly suffers. In these moments, a Bible verse from a well-meaning friend can seem like a weapon wielded (remember Job's buddies?).

Life may never be the same, but it will be worth living again. It was for Carrie, in the wake of such horrors. I've been in a place where I didn't see light at the end of the tunnel—and the tunnel had a train bearing down upon me. God was speaking to me, but His answer was different from my friend's. He gave me the strength to move out of that place, but it was not easy and it was not quick. His answer included an outcome I didn't foresee or desire.

Suffering is part of the human experience, and we grow in compassion and understanding through the pain. If you are stuck in that tunnel, if you don't know which way to turn—rest in Him. Give yourself time to heal and restore, because while the body may restore itself in minimal time, the heart takes much longer. Be still and know that He is God. ✳ *Kristin*

Today's Prayer

Dear Jesus, suffering on earth is troublesome, and though we know our future is with You, some days we wonder if we can take the next step. Please, Lord, restore my heart today. And if there's a friend who needs me, give me eyes to see their pain and put a salve of love and compassion upon their heart. Amen.

Don't Forget the Here and Now

"For I know the plans I have for you," declares the LORD, "plans to prosper you and not to harm you, plans to give you hope and a future."

JEREMIAH 29:11

I've often recounted this verse as the one that carried me through to the other side of ovarian cancer. I was on the treatment table in the hospital when the Lord brought this verse to my heart, promising me a future and a hope, and I clung to that Scripture with steel talons from that moment forward. No one needed to hear that there was a future ahead more than I did.

Something happens to you when you've fought against "the C beast" and emerged to hear those two beautiful words you've been dreaming about: CANCER FREE. I think my friend and coauthor Diann Hunt would probably agree. It changes a person. Your outlook on life shifts, and you stop putting things off so readily. The bigger picture is still important, but your focus becomes much more here-and-now.

I'm a true believer in affirmations. Since Scripture tells us that life and death are in the power of our own tongues, I try to speak life as often as I can. Part of that effort comes in a list of affirmations that I've written down, and I say them aloud after my daily prayers.

"I can do all things through Christ which strengtheneth me" (Philippians 4:13 KJV).

The Lord goes before me, making crooked places straight.

I am thinner, stronger, and healthier today than I was yesterday. (I like to think positively.)

Before any of the others, the first affirmation of the day is always the same: *This is the day the Lord has made. I will rejoice and be glad in it.* It's based on Psalm 118:24. I've said it out loud nearly every day of my life for the past several years; I've read it in the Bible a couple of dozen times or more. And yet I didn't make the connection with the verse that followed until recently. Verse 25 (KJV) adds: "O LORD, I beseech thee, send now prosperity."

David didn't pray that the Lord prosper him eventually or someday. He boldly asked Him to send it *now*, without delay, the sooner the better.

I love that about David. He was a very emotional guy. Despite the fact that he frequently looked into the future for what God would do, he also spent a good bit of the Psalms communing with God about the here and now.

How much better does it get than to serve a God with everything in hand? He promises us a future, but He also concerns Himself with providing hope for today. ✳ *Sandie*

Today's Prayer

Thank You so much, Lord Jesus, for the thoughts You think toward us. Every moment of every day, whether today or next year, Your thoughts revolve around peace, hope, and love for Your children. What a concept! Help us to follow your example. Amen.

Tongue Twister

A gossip betrays a confidence, but a trustworthy man keeps a secret.

PROVERBS 11:13

In my younger years, I knew a woman whose favorite pastime seemed to be gossiping. She gossiped about anything and everything. I'd see her talking to friends, cupping her hand around her mouth and whispering news that appeared to be a "secret," and I'd bristle.

With a background as a legal secretary, I knew the meaning of keeping a confidence. My job depended on it. I couldn't go around yammering about cases brought into our office. In later years, I became a court reporter with plenty of "juicy tales" to tell, but again, extreme confidence was crucial to our business.

This woman hurt people with news that should have been kept private and seemed to delight when others hadn't been privy to stories on which she had the inside scoop. I'd seen the damage her loose tongue had left behind, and I didn't like it one bit.

Still, my gossiping friend taught me a very important lesson.

One day, the Lord seemed to impress upon my heart to pray for her. Oh, I was only too happy to comply. I rolled up my sleeves and went to work on my knees, praying that God would show her just how wrong she was for speaking when she should have been silent—and asking Him to give her what she deserved for her unkind remarks. Soon I realized I wasn't truly praying for her, but rather complaining about her.

The Lord seemed to whisper that I should pray blessings on her, her family, and her job, as though praying for a special friend and wanting God's best for her.

Needless to say, I was less than thrilled with the idea. (And *I* had the nerve to judge *her*?) Yet if God said to do it, I would do it.

So I began to pray for her, as I felt I was being led. I imagine you know what happened. *I* changed. I truly began to see her through different eyes. Her family needs concerned me. I wanted God's best for all of them. Before long, I counted it a privilege to pray for her and her family.

I have no idea if she ever stopped her gossiping ways. It's been many years since I've seen her or her family. But I still have a soft place in my heart for them.

There is a reason God admonishes us not to gossip. It betrays friends and hurts people. The next time you're tempted to do it, don't! And if you know someone who does, pray for them. Pray for them as a true friend; in the end, I believe God will bless you both. ✳ *Diann*

Today's Prayer

Father, Your Son endured insults and knows
how tongues can be weapons of destruction. May my words
offer grace and mercy to others, and may I build up
another in the faith. I love you. Amen.

Indiana Jones Syndrome

Whoever digs a pit may fall into it;
whoever breaks through a wall may be bitten by a snake.

ECCLESIASTES 10:8

Wow! Ecclesiastes 10:8 packs some powerful and graphic words, but it carries so much meaning on a lot of different levels.

As I ponder the visual, I think about one of the ways it can be interpreted, and it's related to being a good neighbor versus a bad one. I live in a planned suburban neighborhood with houses that are fairly close together. We have an active homeowners' association, so it's hard not to know other people's business.

Most of the people on our street behave...usually, anyway. We're a friendly bunch. When people get sick, we bring them fruit or muffins. We stand out in the yard together and stare at the sky, looking for rain clouds during a drought. And we commiserate when it rains so much that the lawn mowers get bogged down in the mud beneath knee-high grass. My husband and I own an extension ladder and a power washer that we swap out with a neighbor who has a fertilizer spreader and an edger. About a dozen houses on our side of the street have the same lawn service, so we get a group discount. This whole neighborhood thing is a nice arrangement when things go well.

Occasionally—and fortunately very rarely—someone stirs up trouble. A rumor starts when a teenager takes advantage of his parents going out of town and throws a party—or someone's spouse suddenly isn't there anymore. Is the child on drugs? Is the couple getting a divorce and breaking up the family? These start out as questions that eventually turn into statements. Whoever starts the rumor is guilty of digging dirt in the neighbor's yard, and if that person isn't careful, it's a deep hole to fall into. And the snakes in the bottom of that hole are all the repercussions of spreading malicious rumors. While it temporarily may be fun to talk about someone, later on, that fun can make matters worse—not only for the subject of the gossip but for the people spreading it.

I love a good story as much as the next person, and I've listened to way more gossip than I should have. As titillating as it may be, it feels dirty and disgusting later on. I know it's not pleasing to God for us to be involved in malicious talk at any level. He makes it very clear how He feels in this verse. I want to wake up each morning feeling refreshed and able to face my day without having to mess with the slimy snakes that come from any pit I have dug in a neighbor's yard. ✳ *Debby*

Today's Prayer

Keep me close to You and in Your Word, Lord Jesus.
Guard me against all the temptations of serpents who find joy
in enticing me with anything impure and unrighteous. Amen.

This Itty-Bitty Light of Mine

When I consider your heavens, the work of your fingers,
the moon and the stars, which you have set in place, what is man that you
are mindful of him, the son of man that you care for him?

PSALM 8:3–4

One of my favorite memories entails a family trip to Cape Hatteras, North Carolina. Our first night there, I joined my kids, nieces, and nephews out on the deck of the house we rented. The house sat right on the beach, so we were able to turn out all the lights and lay there in total darkness, staring up at the vast sky.

Only a few stars twinkled at first, but as our eyes slowly grew accustomed to the dark, more and more stars became evident. In time, the sky was awash in stars. I couldn't help but become mesmerized.

I also couldn't help but feel *really* small.

I'm no science whiz, but even I know that each of those stars, including the ones we couldn't see at first, is like our sun in general size and intensity. Our sun is actually an average-to-small star. But the universe is so huge and those stars are so far away, they only twinkle for us. And that's just *our* galaxy.

Okay, I have to stop there. That's all I remember from *Bill Nye, The Science Guy*. But you get the picture. We can understand why David asked what he did in today's verses: Why us, Lord? Why do we rate Your consideration and care? Your love?

No doubt, as a shepherd David occasionally lay out in the fields and did exactly what I did with the kids that evening in Hatteras. It's difficult to ignore God's majesty when you look at the heavens and understand that He set everything in its place out there. After doing all that, why would He be mindful of little man?

There is amazing honor in the fact that He loves us like that. Regardless of how puny we are in comparison with the rest of creation, He considers us so important He gave His only Child to redeem us.

Ironically, the more we understand that honor, the easier it should be to embrace humility. There's a point to Christian humility. As John the Baptist said of our relationship with Christ, "He must become greater; [we] must become less" (John 3:30). We do a better job of reflecting God's love—Christ's love—when we behave humbly, rather than lording our privileged status over someone. Like the stars at night reflect the light of the sun, we should strive to reflect Christ's light twenty-four hours a day. ✱ Trish

Today's Prayer

Lord, I'm forever amazed by the way You love me.
That's all about You, Lord, so please help me to remain
humble and to shine Your love to others. It would be my honor
to draw others to You through the way I live my life. Amen.

I Am Not Ashamed

*As the Scripture says, "Anyone who trusts in him
will never be put to shame."*

ROMANS 10:11

I wasn't a Christian in college. We had a few kids on our dorm floor who were Christians. We called them the "God Squad," and we made fun of them pretty regularly behind their backs. Nice, huh?

However, there was this gorgeous blond guy at the end of my dorm. I knew he wanted to date me, but he didn't ask, and I used to wonder why. *No ego problems here, I guess.* His door was always open, and he invited anyone in to talk when life was rough.

I had a particularly busy college schedule. I worked two jobs, and I went to school at night and two days during the week. I was dubbed the "Floor Ghost" because I was never in the dorm, and only my roommate knew me well. We were both late-nighters known to run out for Big Gulps in the middle of the night—even with a recent murder one block from our dorm.

Can I just say here that God cares for the least of these? Even when they're ignorant?

Anyway, one dateless Friday night, I wandered by this guy's room on my way home from work, and his door was open. He was listening to music and reading his Bible. When he turned around to face me, I felt *stuck!*...not wanting a sermon but with nowhere to go. I suddenly became like a deer caught in headlights.

"Hi," he said gently, and he invited me in—keeping the door open the entire time I was there. I don't know how long we talked. I can't even remember anything that was said, but I do remember that the conversation had a profound impact on me.

He had a godly peace and warmth about him. Our discussion was very intimate without crossing any boundaries, and I felt unsure about what had transpired. I will not say I fell down and committed my life to the Lord. At least another year passed before that happened.

Whenever I read Romans 1:16—"I am not ashamed of the gospel, because it is the power of God for the salvation of everyone who believes: first for the Jew, then for the Gentile"—this conversation comes back to me. I remember that if I am embarrassed, God is behind me providing the supernatural *oomph* I need to see beyond myself.

To this day, those events in college make no sense to me. Why have they stuck with me? There is only One explanation that I can think of. ✴ *Kristin*

Today's Prayer

Dear Jesus, thank You for speaking to me. Let me be silent
to hear Your voice when I need it today. I pray that, as I go out
in the world and see someone who needs Your warmth, I would
use the supernatural power of the Holy Spirit to speak to them
in the just the right way that they need to hear You.
Let Your light shine before me today. Amen.

Silence Really Can Be Golden

A fool gives full vent to his anger,
but a wise man keeps himself under control.

PROVERBS 29:11

My father used to say that I was a child born in mid-conversation. I always had something to say, no matter what the subject; and in an argument, I simply had to have the final word. It drove my military-officer father straight out of his mind.

"You know," my mother said to me one afternoon following a particularly poorly chosen battle with my father, "there are some people in the world who choose not to express every emotion they have at the very moment they have it. They hold a little something back."

I'm sorry. Foreign-language alert. English, please?

I was around fourteen when we had that conversation. It was a solid couple of decades before I caught up to her thinking, and there was a very long string of repercussions along the way before I got there. As I matured and grew older, however, I learned that words hold a lot of power and sometimes their utterance can set things into motion that can't be stopped.

"I was furious with him," a close friend told me as she paced from the kitchen to the dining room and back again. "I literally saw red. I just remember turning and screaming at him, telling him I couldn't believe what a disappointment he'd become, how I'd never trust him again." And then she'd uttered the words that she wouldn't be able to take back. "I told him to get out of the house, and the sooner the better."

"Christine, he's your son," I reminded her. "You really tossed him out of the house?"

Within ten minutes of her saying the words, things were rolling along behind them and she had no time to snatch them back. Her 17-year-old son had packed a duffel bag and two boxes, loaded them into his car, and pulled out of the driveway. Christine spent every day of the next three years wishing she could take back the anger she'd unleashed on her son and lamenting the fact that she hadn't thought to control her tirade.

I've been praying with Christine since then that her son would come home. Her faith has wobbled now and again, and some days it was just harder to believe that Justin would eventually return. But today I got the call from my friend. Justin walked through the door while Christine and her husband were having their morning coffee.

"He looks like a stranger. I've lost three years because of one moment of uncontrolled anger," she cried. "What a terrible way to learn a lesson!" ✳ *Sandie*

Today's Prayer

Oh Lord, let us all count our lessons as learned before
the damage is done. Help me to hold my tongue in every instance,
at least long enough to think through the consequences. Let Your
spirit of self-control guide my actions and my words. Amen.

True Refreshment

A generous man will prosper;
he who refreshes others will himself be refreshed.

PROVERBS 11:25

$\mathcal{I}$ have a friend who has discovered the secret of today's Scripture. I've never met anyone who thinks of others the way this friend does (well, other than Mother Teresa, whom, incidentally, I have *not* met—though I will meet her in heaven one day). When there is a need, my friend is there. No matter who it is, she will do whatever it takes to help someone. It's in her nature. She has the nature of Jesus.

It amazes me how some people, like my friend, are automatically geared that way. The first thing that seems to pop into their heads is how they can help someone, while others tend to focus on their own problems and never once seem to consider how they might reach out to someone else.

Maybe it's something learned over time by watching parents or friends put others first. Maybe it's strength of character. Or maybe it's Jesus working (though some of us may not be listening).

Sometimes my circumstances scream loudly for attention and it's hard to focus on anything else. I want to wallow in self-pity, down a two-pound bag of M&Ms while watching *Sleepless in Seattle*, and slip into a chocolate-induced coma. During those times, I have to remind myself that there's always someone who has more need than I do. Perhaps that person not only has had a bad day, but they have no M&Ms to get them through it.

Now, lest you think I turn to chocolate instead of the Lord during times of crises, I want you to know that M&Ms, for me, are much more than chocolate. I belong to a group consisting of ladies who call ourselves the M&Ms, which is short for *Monday Mentors*. We started as a Bible study group and have morphed into a once-a-month meeting where we share our life's struggles, joys, and, well, M&Ms (the chocolate ones). We pray together, keep in touch through email, and, in short, put each other's needs above our own. There is nothing I wouldn't do for them.

There is something refreshing about refreshing others. Who can *you* encourage today? Who needs to be reminded that someone cares—that Jesus is reaching out to them in their loneliness, in their need? Maybe you are their hope for better days ahead.

Go on. Forget about yourself. Go out and help someone else. And be sure to take your M&Ms. ✳ *Diann*

Today's Prayer

Father, how I love and adore You. Thank You for the reminder
that we're all in this together. It's not about me; it's about You!
I know that You care about Your children—all of them, as should
we. Help me to keep my focus off my problems and onto the needs
of others. You are my strength and amazing example. Amen.

Here Comes the Judge

"Do not judge, or you too will be judged."

MATTHEW 7:1

He tells us not to judge, or we'll be judged. Oops!

Well, it's sort of too late for me. I've done way more than my share of judging, and it started a long time ago. Like before I had kids, when I saw an unruly toddler throwing a temper-tantrum in a restaurant. "My kid would never do that." *<snort> Right!* Just like my kid would never tell a lie, talk back, or say words that are on our family's "bad words" list. *<snicker>* Those thoughts of having the perfect, well-behaved child faded as soon as my daughters started walking and talking. *And why is that woman scowling at me like that?* Okay, so I admit that my kids could scream along with the best of them. *Sourpuss* must not have kids of her own.

How about the time I saw the guy in the next cubicle cleaning out his desk? What did he do to get the axe? Must've been something terrible for the company not to give him any notice. That judgment lasted for about two days—until everyone in my department was called into a meeting and informed that the company needed to cut back. They were sad to lose one of their most valuable employees, but when he found out there were going to be cutbacks, he volunteered to leave because he was so close to retirement anyway. He didn't want anyone else to lose their jobs. I felt like a rat for judging him when he was willing to give up something for the good of others.

We've been ordered not to judge, but how many people can honestly say they've followed His order? Very few, I bet. Think about it and reflect on how, when we judge, we assume something that is a) none of our business and b) downright wrong. See, that's the thing. Judging others based on assumptions is asking for trouble. We risk our credibility with others when we assume something based on how things look, and God knows the impurity in our hearts when we make assumptions. How dare we judge others when we're just as bad as—or worse than—the people being judged.

One important thing to remember about judging, though, is that we are still to exercise discernment. There is a difference between right and wrong, and we've been given people in positions of authority who may judge based on the laws of the land.

I'm working on looking at others without judging them. It isn't easy for me, but unless I want people to judge me based on incorrect assumptions, I need to do that. ✳ *Debby*

Today's Prayer

Lord Jesus, please give me the discernment I need
without the judgment based on assumptions. You have given me
grace, and I pray that I'm able to follow Your lead. Amen.

Enemies? Who, Me?

As for me, far be it from me that I should sin against the LORD by failing to pray for you. And I will teach you the way that is good and right.

1 SAMUEL 12:23

*D*o you have any enemies? I mean, hard-core enemies? I don't think I do, when I really consider it. Certainly I have the same big-time enemies as the rest of the civilized world—the ones who terrorize for a living. But personally? When I hear Matthew's admonishment to love my enemies, no one in particular comes to mind.

Still, if I ratchet it down a notch to people who put a crimp in my life, who rather passively work against me for one reason or another...there, I suppose, I could come up with a few names. Can you?

I think that was what Samuel addressed in today's verse. He had been asked by his "employers," essentially, to replace himself: to find someone to become king of Israel, to step down as judge, and to not let the door hit him on the backside on his way out. He admonished the Israelites for desiring a king (when they already had *the* King). But then he said he'd be sinning against the Lord if he failed to pray for them.

So these weren't people plotting Samuel's demise. They didn't hate him, as enemies hate. But they demeaned him, rejected him, and treated him unfairly.

Now we're talking. I can *certainly* identify there. How about you? But I can't say I've ever thought, *I need to be sure to pray for [him/her/them]. I'd be sinning against God if I didn't.* But that's what Samuel (and God) says we're to do. Frankly, I'd just as soon I didn't come across this verse.

But I did, and now you did too. If you've been paying attention, you've already identified who that person is (or those people are) in your life. And consider this: you may be the only person in the world praying for that person. Not only is that sad for them, but that's an honor for you. And it also could be why the person is such a pill.

While we're at it, let's broaden the criteria: include the man who'll cut you off in traffic this week; the woman with thirty items in the express aisle; the surly kid with his boxers hanging over his sagging jeans; the girl with the pierced tongue and foul mouth; the next person who makes you frown.... ✳ *Trish*

Today's Prayer

Lord God, far be it from me to refuse to pray for people who trip me up. You know what each of us needs in life. You know what will turn each person's heart to You and give them a desire to live a kind, godly life. Not only do I pray for a spirit of forgiveness in me, but I pray for a hunger for You in them. Amen.

Unwanted Hair

"For the waywardness of the simple will kill them,
and the complacency of fools will destroy them; but whoever listens
to me will live in safety and be at ease, without fear of harm."

PROVERBS 1:32–33

I don't like to be told what to do.

If you know me, you're laughing out loud right now. "Really? You?"

It's a lifelong, recurring theme in my life. If you tell me what to do, I will almost always do the opposite, just to show you how utterly brilliant I am. It's not a positive character trait in any way, shape, or form. And it's much worse in my children, who seem to have caught this anti-establishment gene with vigor.

People like me, people who don't listen to advice, can be annoying, and they're often in need of rescuing. There are simply times (probably most times) when we don't have the whole picture, only a fragment of it, even though we think we do—and that's why God's laws are here for us, set in place for those who will hear. The operative word: WILL. I know it's pride, pure and simple. The Bible says that pride (haughty eyes—*ugh, the description!*) is one of those ugly sins, the kind that God hates. In fact, He uses it to describe the way he felt about hairy Esau.

Unwanted hair—I so get that. It's hateful! (I'm Italian.) And it is painful to remove, just like the sins we're not willing to part with. That's what pride is like to God: *unwanted body hair.* So why do I do it? Time and time again, why do I look up and say, "But wait! I think I have a better idea!"

The thing about unwanted hair (and sin) is that it comes back if you're not diligent. Sometimes I look back at those moments and see God there, shaking His head and saying to His angels, "Get out the hot wax and muslin strips. She's at it again."

So when you think you have way too much to do in a day, when there's just not enough time to drag out the wax and get serious about removing what shouldn't be there...that's the day to get on your knees. Do the work and remove the unwanted from your life.

Imagine the world we'd have if we all did as we were told. It would be a much nicer place to live. ✳ *Kristin*

Today's Prayer

Dear Lord in heaven, help me to see the ways I run
from Your laws and the ways I prove my folly and foolishness
every day. Your ways were set in place for my benefit, Lord.
To do it my way is not cute; it is sin. Remind me, Lord, that sin
is ugly while Your Word is beautiful. It is life, and it's there
for my own protection. Forgive me my transgressions
and help me to be better today.

Kicking the Habit

Submit yourselves, then, to God. Resist the devil,
and he will flee from you.

JAMES 4:7

I read somewhere that it takes at least two solid weeks of repetition before a habit is established, and I used that theory when I tried (for the third time in my life) to quit smoking. I decided that every time the craving swooped in, I would replace it with a prayer and a replacement taste; I landed on a lip-pursing can (or two) of diet orange soda and a Scripture to which I could cling: "Resist the devil, and he will flee from you."

For the first week, you could have sliced cheese on my razor-sharp nerves, and I'm sure beverage stock went up as I consumed soda after soda. But I just kept at it, promising myself that the cravings would flee. Eventually. One day. *Please, God.*

Halfway through the second week, however, I couldn't stand it any longer. I got into my car, drove to the nearest convenience store, and bought a pack of cigarettes. I couldn't wait until I got home, so I peeled the package open before I even started the car. I held the package to my nose and breathed in deeply. There it was! The familiar draw of nicotine.

I rummaged through my purse and was horrified to discover that I'd tossed out my last disposable lighter in a moment of perceived resolution. The spot once-upon-a-time occupied by a cigarette lighter on the dashboard was now a wide open *O* next to the radio. Trying to decide between sprinting back into the store for a light and driving home for one, I caught a glimpse of myself in the rearview mirror. My unlit enemy sagged from my tight lips, and the scowl spread over my entire face like an angry Halloween mask. I looked myself in the eyes for a full minute before I pulled the cigarette from my mouth and crushed it in my hand. With frustrated resolve, I stalked to the trash can on the curb and deposited my purchase into it.

It wasn't until I floated into the third week on an orange-carbonated sea that I began to glimpse hope on the horizon beyond my nicotine fantasies. On the nineteenth day of my battle, I'd already had breakfast and headed for the office before I realized I hadn't yet given a single thought to a cigarette—or a can of orange soda, for that matter. I remember laughing right out loud at the discovery, and the guy next to me at the stoplight looked at me as if I'd escaped from the asylum. Which, in a way, I suppose I had. ✷ *Sandie*

Today's Prayer

Thank You, Lord, for giving us the sword of Your Word to cling to when the battle rages—and for helping us to hang on just a little bit longer when it clearly looks like we can't. Amen.

When She Spoke, We Listened

Reckless words pierce like a sword,
but the tongue of the wise brings healing.

PROVERBS 12:18

Someone once said, "The only difference between you now and you five years from now is the books you read and the people you meet."

No doubt about it, other people influence us and we influence other people—in good *and* bad ways. The people who come to mind first for me when thinking of influencers are teachers.

We've all had our share of good and bad teachers, though maybe we judge the good and the bad of it by different criteria—she didn't teach well, she yelled all the time, and so on.

I had a third-grade teacher whom I well remember to this day. And let me just say for the record, I'm not yet on Social Security, but I *am* past menopause, just so you know. In other words, *third grade was a long time ago.*

The thing that struck me most about Mrs. Burton, aka *Teacher Extraordinaire*, was her soft voice. I don't ever remember her raising her voice. There were days when we tested her patience, I'm sure. Maybe, if I tried real hard, I could remember a frown or two when we were a tad too energetic. But I never, ever remember her raising her voice.

Anytime she walked past my desk, she may as well have been Mother Teresa. Yes, I thought that much of her. She was my hero. I loved just being around her because she was kind and gentle. Her presence brought comfort and inner happiness to me.

There could have been any number of reasons for her soft voice, of course. A yearlong bout with laryngitis. A determination to set an example so we would keep our voices down. But somehow my little third-grade brain knew it was much more than that.

Turns out, I was right.

Later, when I reached high school, I visited a church with my friend...and who do you suppose was a regular member? That's right, Mrs. Burton. No wonder I'd sensed something extra special about her. It was her love for the Lord that shone through and opened the eyes of this third grader to a tenderness I'd rarely seen in others. Her gentle, encouraging words impacted my life in ways I can hardly quantify. Without even knowing it, she challenged me to make a difference with my words in my corner of the world.

How about you? At day's end, if you played back the words you used on any given day, would they be words that build up or tear down? Let's pray that God will use our words to bring healing and encouragement in the heart of another today. ✳ *Diann*

Today's Prayer

Father, how I praise You for Your example of ultimate love.
Help me to offer healing and love through my words
to others today and every day. Amen.

Busy, Busy, Busy

In the beginning God created the heavens and the earth.

GENESIS 1:1

"I have so much to do today," I whined to my husband one morning. "I have three loads of laundry to wash, dry, and fold. Then I have to write at least one chapter, or I won't make my deadline, and I have to write an article."

"Yeah, I'm busy too." My husband paused for a couple of seconds by the door then glanced at his watch. "I have a client coming in first thing this morning, and I have to prepare for him. But I have a feeling I'm forgetting something." He nodded toward a file he'd placed on the kitchen island. "Oh, there it is. Would you mind getting that for me? My hands are full."

I grabbed his file and followed him out to his car. After he got situated with his files, coffee, and lunch bag, he headed off to work while I went inside to toss some clothes into the washing machine before sitting down at my computer.

Wally and I have become so busy with all our "work," we often feel like we're forgetting something. Busy, busy, busy. That night, we sat down to eat dinner in silence, too exhausted to talk.

As I consider the things I do each day and how much importance I place on each little task, I realize it's nothing compared to what God did in one single day. God created the heavens and the earth in the time it took me to write a chapter of a book and do laundry. If I skipped laundry that day, the worst thing that would have happened is we'd have to wear clothes stuck in the back of the drawer. Imagine what would have happened if God had skipped creating either heaven or earth. I obviously wouldn't be worried about laundry, would I?

If we held up our tasks next to what God has done for us, we'd always feel insignificant, but He doesn't see it that way. He knows each of us, and we're all important to him. Our laundry? Not so much. Finishing a chapter of a book? Nah. But our souls matter. God's power is humongous. He prepared a place for us to live and learn about Him. He gave us the work we do, but the stress we feel is self-imposed. I can only imagine how Wally and I would freak out if we were assigned God's to-do list. *Create heavens—check. Create earth—check.* By the time we finished with that, we'd have to live in total darkness for a very long time before we summoned the energy to move on to creating light. ✱ *Debby*

Today's Prayer

Lord, heavenly Father, thank You for preparing a place
for each of your children. I pray that I am able to put my own life
into perspective and to fully acknowledge Your holiness. Amen.

His Word

Then the woman said to Elijah, "Now I know that you are a man of God and that the word of the LORD from your mouth is the truth."

1 KINGS 17:24

Lately I've intently sought God's guidance regarding some decisions that will significantly impact my future security. I haven't yet heard His answer, so I vented to a couple of my girlfriends the other night. "God knows I'm wide-open to whatever path He wants me to take with this. I just wish there wasn't all this *mystery* to it! I'm listening as hard as I can. Why doesn't He just *tell* me what He wants me to do?"

Even though both friends nodded in empathy, one of them said, "That's just not the way He works, is it? He's a 'lamp unto our feet.' No farther than that."

We decided God knows our wayward hearts. He knows that if we see too far ahead, we'll cast him a jaunty salute, say a quick thanks, and turn our backs to get on with our business. By only granting us a lamp unto our feet, He keeps us looking up for more light all through the journey, which is exactly what we faulty creatures need to do to stay on the straight and narrow. In that way He's truly a light unto our path.

Today's verse highlights a point in time when the prophet Elijah followed the lamp at his feet. During a drought he followed it into a ravine, where he had water for a time and God had ravens bring him food. *Ravens.* You don't plan something like that. But God did.

Then Elijah followed the lamp to a widow making a final loaf of bread for her son and herself, after which she expected to die of starvation. The last thing she needed was another dinner guest. You *certainly* don't plan that kind of visit (if you have manners). But God did. Elijah assured the widow that God would work it out. And with God's provision, the three of them had bread every day.

Then the widow's son became ill and died. She blamed Elijah and his God. Elijah saw no lamp for his feet to follow. Still, he took the boy from her, expressed his utter frustration to God, and lay across the boy. Why? Maybe after following the lamp for a while, we start to understand what we need to do even when the path isn't well-lit. Elijah's desperate prayer on the boy's behalf led to his resurrection.

So I'll keep watching that lamp at my feet and trust that, if things become so desperate I just lay myself before Him and pray, He'll very likely breathe new life and light unto my path. ✳ *Trish*

Today's Prayer

Lord, Your Word is the only light I need to follow.
Please help me remember to come back to that light before
every step on the path You've set before me. Amen.

Word Up!

Whoever of you loves life and desires to see many good days,
keep your tongue from evil and your lips from speaking lies.

PSALM 34:12–13

It's scientifically proven that positive words have a positive effect on us as humans. In fact, using negative words has been shown to lead to immediate negative results on the body and our overall mood. If we continually use negative words, they can zap our spirit, our emotional strength, and our self-confidence.

When reading books about abused women for a novel I wrote, I was astonished to find that emotional abuse leaves a deeper scar than physical abuse. Why? Because emotional abuse goes to the very heart of what makes up the essence of that person. It tells them they're unworthy and of no value.

Sticks and stones may break your bones, but words can destroy you. Don't underestimate the value of what a kind word can do for someone today.

This morning, my daughter had horseback riding camp. She begged me not to get coffee first. "Mom, no! We'll be late!"

"I won't go to Starbucks," I told her. "I'll go the local shop. It won't take so long."

Naturally, I got to talking to the owner, and my daughter was soon yanking me by the arm.

"See? You have to talk to everyone!" she exclaimed as we left.

And I do.

The owner told me the business was having trouble with the city and may be closed by the end of this year. How could I not offer words of encouragement and my own experience in dealing with the city?

My daughter made it on time, incidentally. I've developed the ability to account for my chatty nature and leave early. But when you talk as much as I do, it isn't always positive.

Sometimes I blow it. Trust me, it's harder to make up for harsh words than it is to say something kind. They say that a bad experience will be shared seven times, but a good one is only conveyed to someone else once. Now, with Twitter and Facebook, I imagine that number is multiplied! I like to think of our words as echoing to the world. Are we sending a pretty, uplifting echo?

Consider the way you use words. God promises us more good days and a longer life if we keep our tongue from evil. That's a pretty big reward for something that might come naturally to us as we practice, but the Bible tells us that the tongue is a fire, a world of evil among the parts of the body, so we must constantly check ourselves and be mindful of our words. ✱ *Kristin*

Today's Prayer

Dear Jesus, thank You for giving me the ability to connect with people around me through words. I pray that You would help me to always uplift and shine Your light into the world with my tongue. Help me to bring joy and encouragement to those around me, just as You would. Amen.

Bridge Over Troubled Moving Vans

"For my yoke is easy and my burden is light."

MATTHEW 11:30

When word finally came back that everything was in order and approved and I was actually going to take ownership of the house I wanted, a whole new set of challenges arose for me. I realized I was going to have to actually *MOVE!*—even though I was in pretty precarious physical health.

I wasn't too worried at first because I'd put together a plan, and anyone who knows me knows how much I love a good plan! I have several local friends who would no doubt offer an hour here or there to help me pack, who would perhaps be willing to help me move things around to keep it orderly. After all, when Carrie Bradshaw moved, her friends made it a three-day group affair, right?

You know the dividend of assumptions, right? Not one of those friends offered to help at all. I was stunned. There were family commitments and tight schedules and basic life to take care of, and my struggles were left completely to my own devices to solve. Suddenly this massive blessing for which I was so grateful transformed into one of the biggest burdens of my life. I was completely overwhelmed. Wasn't the burden supposed to be *light*?

One evening, my childhood friend, Marian, called from Ohio. "I was thinking I might fly down around the time of the move," she said, "so I can be there to help you get settled." And of course I immediately burst into tears. I'm a crier. That's how I roll.

The rest of the work in preparation for the move seemed easier somehow, just by knowing that on the other end, Marian would be there. The night before the moving van was to arrive, I sat in my car at the airport as I waited for her flight to land and held back another flow of grateful tears.

Once we were back at the old house and surrounded by boxes, Marian and I chattered on about my hopes for the new place. And before we turned in for the night, my precious friend asked me, "What do you need me to do tomorrow before the movers come?"

There's an old saying about a burden shared no longer being an actual burden. Marian is the embodiment of that truth. By thinking with her heart and listening with her spirit, she unselfishly answered a need for me that eased my considerable load.

Before she left to go back to Ohio, I asked her if she knew she'd been the manifestation of answered prayer. She simply smiled. I don't think she'd really thought of it that way, which of course makes her all the more special as the answer to my prayers. ✳ *Sandie*

Today's Prayer

Lord, thank You so much for orchestrating
solutions to our burdens. Please bless those instruments
of Your work, like Marian, by always providing
an easy yoke for them as well. Amen.

A Fresh Slate

Because of the LORD's great love we are not consumed, for his compassions never fail. They are new every morning; great is your faithfulness.

My husband is an elementary school teacher. When September rolls around each year, he is as excited as his students. We go shopping for clothes and school supplies, and he gets his room ready for the kids. The smell of sharpened pencils, fresh chalk, and cleaning supplies fill the room. New wall hangings, posters, clean blackboards, and a tidy desk all mark the beginning of a school year.

Each year, he learns something from the year before—which tools strike interest in the hearts of the students, what presentations worked and which ones flopped. He considers new ways to motivate the day-dreamers and challenge the restless. He takes his newfound knowledge into the next year in hopes of doing a better job than before.

Some days he comes home and feels as though he didn't accomplish a thing. Other days he wonders how he could ever do any other job. Every class offers new challenges of its own, and my husband faces each one head-on, with renewed encouragement and excitement for another year.

In short, he gets a fresh slate.

When my kids were little, I wanted to be just like Caroline Ingalls. You know, kindness lifting from my lips like a soft minuet and wisdom rolling into every word. Unfortunately, it didn't work like that for me.

There were days when the kids were rowdy and I had a headache— I don't think Caroline ever had those. My patience was short and the tone of my voice carried around the block like a marine corps sergeant. Unfortunately, I resembled Mrs. Oleson more than I did Mrs. Ingalls.

I prayed for wisdom, gentleness, and, yes, even patience. So many nights I wondered what kind of memories I had created for my children that day. I'd fall on my knees and pray, "Lord, help them to forget everything I did wrong and remember if I did anything right." It must have worked. They speak fondly of their childhood.

Some days are hard. The challenges seem too great to bear. Sometimes we can't seem to work beyond our past. We feel that God is silent and we're all alone. But then His Word reminds us that His compassions never fail. They are new every morning! Great is His faithfulness!

Forget about yesterday. *This* is the day that the Lord has made. You have the opportunity to start all over. Trust God with it. Go into a hurting world and make brand-new memories—memories that matter. You have a fresh slate. Go with His blessings. ✻ *Diann*

Today's Prayer

Father, thank You for each new day where I can learn
to trust You more. May I be counted among the obedient, the
faithful. Help me to make the most of every opportunity and to
remember that your compassions are new every morning.

Where's the Beef?

*Better a meal of vegetables where there is love
than a fattened calf with hatred.*

PROVERBS 15:17

When I made the announcement to my husband that we were going to try for "meatless Mondays"—at least most of the time—to cut back on fatty foods and save a little money in the process, he didn't balk. In fact, he seemed to think it was a good idea. He knew I was doing it as an act of self-improvement rather than in trying to deny him the rich taste of meat with every meal. I'm sure this wasn't what the Lord meant by this verse, but there is something to be said for cutting back, as long as it's done with love.

For a while, almost everyone I knew was grabbing everything within their reach—whether they could afford it or not. If there was room on their credit cards, they could buy the latest and greatest—shiny new cars, jewelry, clothes, houses.... When their kids wanted something, all they had to do was stick out their hands and suddenly a plastic card would appear. Why should parents deny their offspring whatever their hearts desired? Their human wants were temporarily satisfied, but when the next shiny thing came along...well...you know. Is that really love?

Hard times have since fallen on many families, and they've had to pull back and tighten up. When their children ask why they suddenly have to sacrifice anything, the once-indulgent parents are left trying to figure out how to explain true values. They may have been forced to sell their mini-mansions and move into smaller homes where they—*<gasp!>*—are forced to be in the same room with each other. This is something that would have been so much easier if they'd done that to begin with.

The Lord in His wisdom knew that a feast of everything we could possibly want would fill us temporarily, but later we'd be hungry again.

No matter how much we have, there will always be an emptiness that can't ever be totally satisfied. However, a less-ostentatious meal of sharing His good news will last forever, leaving us satisfied and never hungering for more. After all, what more could anyone want besides living in His kingdom for eternity?

Joy fills me as I know His plan for me is richer and much more nourishing than anything I could ever satisfy myself with. When my husband and I sit down to a meal without meat, we're just as happy as we'd be if we had the thickest, juiciest steaks. It's not the food that brings us true joy but knowing that we have each other and the Lord is with us at every moment of our day. ✳ *Debby*

Today's Prayer

Dear Lord, thank You for richly blessing my family
with the joy of Your greatness. I pray that I'll continue to focus
on the truly rich meal of Your Word rather than the
skimpiness of worldly desires. Amen.

Love, Hope, and Faith

Not only so, but we also rejoice in our sufferings,
because we know that suffering produces perseverance;
perseverance, character; and character, hope.
And hope does not disappoint us,
because God has poured out his love into our hearts
by the Holy Spirit, whom he has given us.

ROMANS 5:3–5

*D*o you remember the first time your heart was broken? I had to dig through the old memory to remember getting dumped the first time, but I found the little gem hiding in a far-off corner. I can't dredge up the pain I felt back then, but I remember feeling it. It was devastating. The truly odd thing is that the pain of that first heartbreak seemed more searing than the pain of having a marriage pulled out from under me after nearly two decades. Was I really that cold about my marriage?

Quite the opposite. I didn't rejoice about the end of my marriage— but after a life's worth of romance and breakup, my devastation has been replaced by hope. Not necessarily hope for more romance, mind you. Simply hope. Because after suffering through multiple heartbreaks, I discovered I could *survive* them, I could persevere. And learning to persevere built my character. Part of my character today is the result of experiencing heartbreak and surviving it. And surviving loss. And surviving failure. And surviving...[fill in the blank]. God designed us to develop multifaceted characters. Knowing He cares enough to improve my character gives me hope.

So it is with all suffering. Regardless of how Paul phrased it, he surely wasn't saying that "real" Christians dance for joy when they learn they have serious illnesses or they lose loved ones or they get laid off or any number of awful turns our lives can take. But the longer we live, the greater the opportunity we have to develop hindsight and wisdom...and hope.

So often we hear people say things like, "I would never have asked for this to happen to me, but I wouldn't change a thing because it made me who I am today." That might sound trite, but the insinuation is that the person *appreciates* who she is today. For a Christian, that means she sees God's hand in her life. She has hope for a God-ordained future.

That kind of hope won't disappoint us. It eventually rises to the surface, despite any suffering we experience, if we persevere and allow our sufferings to build our strength and character.

What does it take for us to believe that hope won't disappoint us? To believe that hope will arrive, and to believe it so strongly that we'll eventually rejoice in our sufferings? Well, it takes faith. When you think of it, that's really the only gift we can give the Lord. It's all He's ever asked of us. ✳ Trish

Today's Prayer

Lord Jesus, You know what I struggle with today.
Please give me the strength to persevere, to be strong in
character, and to always hope in You. Amen.

Shame, Shame, Go Away

No one whose hope is in you will ever be put to shame.

When I read this verse, the image of the biblical Noah comes to me. Noah, in the middle of the desert, building a giant boat, bringing in his own petting zoo two by two (or by seven, if you count the "clean" animals), then packing up what would be the equivalent of a massive Costco run onboard. Can you imagine what the neighbors said? Can you imagine their mocking laughter and pointing fingers? What was it like to be his family during this time? How did they explain God's still, small voice in their father's ear?

The short answer is, they didn't. How could they? If Noah lived today, he'd probably be under psychiatric care and on some pretty heavy doses of medication.

The Bible, however, doesn't talk about the neighbors, except to say that the earth was corrupt and filled with violence. We're told that Noah was a righteous man, blameless among the people of his time, and he simply did *all that God commanded him.*

I'm sure that when the rains started, those folks left on earth had a different view of the odd man building an ark in the desert. Something tells me Noah took no pleasure in being right, but he had to be grateful for his obedience.

I have a special-needs child. One day, we were in Target and that child threw a fit the size of Montana. My other three kids looked on in horror as I tried to calm my child and get out of the store without any major damage. Looking into my other kids' eyes, I saw the shame and humiliation—and I saw the way they stepped back, not wanting to be associated with their sibling.

Through their eyes, I saw myself as a child watching my mother handle my handicapped brother in some overwhelmingly embarrassing situation, and a light came on for me that day. My mother was not ashamed because she loved my brother, and she was focused on the moment and his needs. I felt the same about my child at that moment. There was no shame because I was focused in love.

God did not give me this child by accident. There are many days when I could have easily been put to shame but chose to focus instead on the incredible gift of this child. I've watched my kid blossom and overcome disabilities I didn't think possible to overcome. That is God's grace. That is God saying, "Kristin, build the ark and don't worry about what the neighbors are saying. Your walk isn't theirs."

Someday, my kids will learn this lesson for themselves. There is never any shame in obedience. ✳ *Kristin*

Today's Prayer

Dear Jesus, thank You for giving me the ability to look
past what others think and focus on You. This is an hourly battle,
so I pray that You would keep me close today and help me to
focus on the plan You have laid out for my life. Amen.

Wham, Bam, and Done!

A man's wisdom gives him patience;
it is to his glory to overlook an offense.

PROVERBS 19:11

$\mathcal{I}$ have a secret nickname for one of my friends. I've never said it out loud; it's just something that pops into my head whenever she calls me.

Wham-Bam is a great girl. She's very funny, and she can be so compassionate. But at least once a week, I receive a phone call from her that goes something like this:

ME: Hello?
W-B: Hi, how are you doing?
ME: I'm okay, I guess. Just very tired. I—
W-B: I was up all night three nights in a row because the kids...

She talks about 80 miles per hour as she tells me all about her own life, moving directly into why she called, and then why she has to run.

After about a year of keeping a mental accounting of these calls, I started to take offense. I often pictured that cartoon character that whirled into view and mowed down anyone who came across his path before moving on without looking back at the poor Joe sitting on his duff in the middle of the road, dazed and wondering what had just happened. *Wham-Bam is the Tasmanian Devil!*

More often than not, I've had to really fight the temptation to speak up: "Why do you even call me? You never listen to what I have to say! Am I just the dumping ground when you need to vent?" One evening I turned to the Lord with the questions instead. In that instant, I had what Oprah calls a "lightbulb moment."

How many times had I done the same thing to the Lord during prayer? How many times had I clamped my eyes shut and started a dissertation somewhere in the middle without taking the time to enter into relationship with Him, without thanking Him for the many blessings He had bestowed? At least once a week, I'm certain. Probably more often still.

I started to pray for Wham-Bam that night. I prayed that she would find peace, that her frantic life of carpools and family illness and veterinary bills wouldn't overtake her, and that somewhere in the midst of the chaos, she would find the time to be still before the Lord and trust Him to take care of her every concern.

The next time I received a call from her, I empathized with her predicament, and I told her that I'd been praying for her. Her response? She burst into tears and thanked me. "You know, that's just what I need," she told me. "To know someone is hearing me and praying for me." ✳ *Sandie*

Today's Prayer

Lord, thank You for the countless times You have provided a strong shoulder and a listening ear when I needed to vent, without keeping an account. Help me to provide that for the people around me, and use me to lead them back to the One waiting to hear anything they have to say. Amen.

All That *and* Toilet Paper?

Then he climbed into the boat with them,
and the wind died down. They were completely amazed,
for they had not understood about the loaves;
their hearts were hardened.

MARK 6:51-52

Like many newlyweds, we struggled financially when we were first married. Six months into wedded bliss, we found ourselves needing groceries. Being young and full of faith, we decided we would tell no one... but God.

Several days into this, as our stomachs growled and the food cabinet grew bare, I got a call from a friend wanting to know if I would go shopping with her. The last thing I wanted to do was go shopping. We barely had enough to put a meal together; shoes were the last thing on my mind. Yet, not wanting to spoil her enthusiasm and also not wanting to let on that there was a problem, I quickly agreed.

Once I hung up the phone, I asked God for strength and grace to go shopping with my friend—and for help to keep our need from her. We wanted to rely totally upon God for this need.

So I got dressed and ready to go. My spirits perked as I thought about spending some time with my friend and enjoying our day.

When she showed up at the front door, she had a paper sack filled with groceries in her hands. I opened the door and she walked inside, heading straight for my table. She plunked the groceries on the table and turned to me. "I know this seems crazy, but during my quiet time this morning, the Lord told me you needed this." Then she marched back to her car and brought in several more bags of groceries—right down to paper towels and toilet paper!

God had thought of everything.

I'll never forget that day. We hadn't told a soul of our need. We were careful to not let on to anyone that we had a problem. I don't know if we were putting God to the test or just plain trusting, but He came through for us. The thing that I hadn't expected was how surprised we were. We say we trust Him, so why is it we are amazed when He comes through for us?

God met our need that day—and has every day since then.

Do you have a need? Have you given it over to Him? God uses His people to reach out to others. It doesn't hurt to share your need—unless He tells you to do otherwise. But no matter how you handle it, He is there for you. Trust Him. He's a *BIG* God. ✳ *Diann*

Today's Prayer

Father, thank You that You are so much bigger
than any need we have. Thank You for understanding our fears
and for the strength You provide in times of challenge. Help me
also to be an extension of Your hands to others in need.

I Want What I Want

The LORD is my shepherd, I shall not be in want.

PSALM 23:1

ake what's yours before someone else gets it." "You deserve the best of everything." "Be tough and stand up for yourself." "Whoever amasses the most toys wins." "Be assertive." With thinking like this, who needs God? We can make our own destiny by following the rules of the rich and famous. All we have to do is watch a few reality shows on TV, take notes, and do what they do.

I have to admit that I've been guilty of watching some of these shows. I'm amazed by the sheer opulence I see. I'm also appalled by the train-wreck lives some of them have and how they are rewarded for mis-behavior. (Shh! Don't tell anyone—that's part of what draws me.) Sure, everyone knows it's important to behave—at least when people are look-ing. Or if we have a good reason and a TV camera captures the moment, it's okay to misbehave. According to the laws of the land, we're good citizens if we don't murder, steal, or cheat. Some of the older rules included marital fidelity and respect toward others, but as nonbelievers take over, the rules change.

Following God's plan seems to be an outdated way to live, based on what we see on TV. We're challenged to follow a format that seems attractive and exciting on the outside, but beneath the outward appeal is a sinful motive of self-indulgence in whatever feels good. I think it's obvious that, deep down, most people feel empty with this type of thinking.

As people ridicule the Bible and God's Word, I'm deeply saddened by the bitterness their lack of belief in the Savior has caused. On the sur-face, their point seems valid. They look at Christ and how He's described: humble servant; always loving; never sinned; born in a stable to out-cast parents; filled with sorrow; a crown of thorns. So they ask, "Huh?

This is the King we're supposed to follow?" They wonder what happened to the glorious splendor befitting royalty: purple robes and golden sashes; an ornate throne; a crown with gemstones so heavy a common person would get a headache from it; promises of special favors if we suck up; power; prestige; famous people on speed dial. In their world, God's Word is falling on deaf ears to anyone who isn't willing to look past the shell of righteousness.

Occasionally, I think about how fun it would be to trade places with people who live the trendy lifestyle of shallow perfection. But as I look closer, I see that the joy of knowing Christ is missing. ✳ *Debby*

Today's Prayer

Lord, thank You for filling me with Your Word
and the life You have chosen for me. I pray that sinners
who denounce You will come to You through Christ
and that they'll be filled with the blessings only
You can provide. Amen.

For When You Go Batty

Commit to the LORD whatever you do, and your plans will succeed.

PROVERBS 16:3

How do you know when you're following God's plan for you?

When the UPS man handed me the first copy of my first published book, you'd have thought I'd jump up and down with joy, wouldn't you? Not this girlfriend! Rather, I stood there, holding that book, and experienced a momentary flood of freak-out.

What am I doing? What if my loved ones and friends read this novel and think I stink on ice? What if I never get another book idea? Who am I fooling? Did I misunderstand God's plan for me? How will I know if I'm getting it wrong? Will He use mean reviews and a public shunning to communicate His message? Will He smite me thusly? I don't want to be smote! I don't do well with smiting!

After all these years, I know to stop and pray whenever I go batty like that. I'm telling you, you'll never go wrong with prayer. Like Jell-O, there's always room for it. And in this particular situation, He gave me immediate peace. This time He blessed me with this thought:

"If you commit to Me whatever you do, I will never stomp on your efforts to honor Me. I'm not saying there won't be bumps in the road, but if you commit to Me whatever you do, and I want you to do something else—no worries, dear—I'll lovingly guide you to that something else. I'll lift up in you a desire to do that something else. I love that you want to honor Me. So commit to Me whatever you do, pay attention to what drives you, and then go for it!"

The comforting aspect of such a thought is that, yes, my plans will succeed because eventually He'll make my plans the same as His.

Do you find yourself in flux about decisions, big and small, immediate and long-term? Are you trying to live the life He planned for you but feeling confused about what that entails? Do you struggle to know whether something in your life is God's guidance or simply the hard knocks of life? Or the blessings of life? If you'll take the time each morning to commit to God everything you do that day, you can rest in His promise. Your plans might change. Or they might not unfold exactly as you expected. But they will most definitely succeed. ✳ Trish

Today's Prayer

Lord, I know You love me—You prove that in so many ways, the most important of which is the salvation You give me through the sacrifice of Your Son. I want to honor Your love by following the plans You have for me during my time here on earth. So please help me, Lord, to remember to commit to You whatever I do, each and every day, and then to watch for Your loving guidance. Amen.

True Fulfillment

A man can do nothing better than to eat
and drink and find satisfaction in his work.

ECCLESIASTES 2:24

Wealth is flaunted in front of us every day. As an advertising major in college and a marketing director before becoming a writer, my job was to sell people the dream.

As I've gotten older, I realize how ridiculous that dream is. One doesn't have to look far to see empty lives in gilded cages. Everyone on this earth needs a purpose, and looking half your age is not really a purpose. It's a nice gift but, ultimately, it makes your life no richer. Without purpose, we search to be filled; but without a mission, we are merely wanderers in the desert, hoping in vain to find the elusive oasis and drink heartily from its pool.

Living through the dot-com bust, I watched friends become multi-millionaires...but lives didn't really change that much. People's houses got bigger, maybe their kids went to better schools, but in the end, what was important to them was important to all of us. Money made no difference in their quality of life at all. They had more, but they had more to worry about.

When you know what you're about, making the right choices becomes easier and you can't be sold a bill of goods by a skilled marketing magnate. Once, I wrote a book born out of passion and zeal for a subject close to my heart. I partnered with a publisher on the project, and it didn't work out. Our missions did not coincide. In the end, after trying to make a square peg fit into a round hole, we mutually decided the book belonged elsewhere.

It was a costly decision, not only in time, which I didn't have to lose, but also in finances, which I also didn't have. But because of my purpose, my passion for the book, it was easy to walk away and do the right thing. I answer to Him, and I thought that answer would be compromised if the book was written the way this publisher's mission required. I notice that when I look around me to see what everyone else is doing and compare myself, it's a lot more difficult to do what God is calling me to do.

In the end, God will replace the years the locusts have eaten. He has proven that time and time again. I can look upon the time as wasted, or I can look upon it as a lesson learned, a reminder to stay on the path God has ordained for me. At the end of it, there is nothing better than to be in His will and find satisfaction in my work. The cherry on top is fellowship and food. ✳ *Kristin*

Today's Prayer

Dear Lord, thank You for providing me with purpose
in my lifetime. Please help me to stay on track and to
seek Your will in all that I endeavor to do—in this
day and in those that follow. Amen.

BFFs

"The LORD your God will be with you wherever you go."

JOSHUA 1:9

One of the beauty parts of living alone is that I have developed a very tight relationship with Jesus Christ, so I'm never really by myself. When I'm making breakfast in the morning, I talk to Him about the day ahead, and on the drive to work I often sing to Him at the top of my key-challenged voice; He doesn't even seem to mind the klunker notes! When coworkers get the best of me, when the salad I order has wilted lettuce, when some Joe cuts in front of me in line at Starbucks...He's the Friend to whom I turn. There's nothing I can't say to Him. He knows my darkest secrets as well as my deepest desires.

Yep, me and the Lord, *we'relikethis*.

In fact, He's such a comfortable, familiar Companion in my every-day life that I can sometimes forget that He is the awesome Maker of the universe, the Holy One of Israel, the Anointed One, the Author of our very faith. There is nothing He doesn't know, no place on earth we can go where He can't find us; He knew all our days before even one of them passed, and He numbers every hair on our heads.

I was watching one of those entertainment shows a few days ago, and they were interviewing an A-List movie star. She spoke about her children. Her youngest is around two years old, so she's lived all her life with the paparazzi following the family everywhere they go; however, her older daughter, a teenager, had a relatively normal childhood until the last couple of years. So when Mom was suddenly surrounded on the red carpet or followed down every inch of Melrose while shopping, the teen-ager was appalled.

"Sometimes I think she forgets that there's this whole other side to Mom now," the actress explained. "I'm not just the person she baked cookies with on Saturday...or who scrubbed the grape jelly off her back-pack. I'm also someone who makes movies, and with that comes this sort of celebrity. Sharing me with her little sister was hard enough, but sharing me with the rest of the world isn't something she'd ever consid-ered before."

That resonated in me. God has numbered the hairs on your head as well as mine; and my Jehovah Jirah provides for you too. Despite the deeply personal relationship we share, it's important for me to acknowl-edge the enormity of this personal Savior of mine and to take time to bow down before Him to worship the awesome God that He is. Beyond being my closest Friend, He is so much more. ✳ *Sandie*

Today's Prayer

Lord Jesus, help me to never forget the greatness of Your love...
not just for me, but for everyone around me and all throughout
the world. Wherever I go, You go with me. But not just
with me. We truly are a "family of God." Amen.

It Takes More Than Chocolate

All the days of the oppressed are wretched,
but the cheerful heart has a continual feast.

PROVERBS 15:15

When I'm in a good mood, I feel festive, energetic, ready to meet my day's goals. When my mood goes south, I want to go to bed—and all those around me want me to go to bed too.

Let's face it. We don't *feel* happy every minute of the day. Sometimes we have bad hair days (or in my case, bad wig days). And what woman doesn't get in a bad mood when she's having a bad hair day?

It's true that we don't live in a constant Pollyanna attitude. But we can choose to make the best of our days. As Christians, regardless of how we *feel*, we can have inner joy that holds us steady when life throws chaos our way. It's a joy that says, "Regardless of the circumstances, I choose to trust God to get me through this."

When the doctor told me I had ovarian cancer, it took awhile for that to sink in. I didn't immediately fall apart or get depressed. I was in a state of shock and disbelief. Once the news did sink in (as I was getting my hair shaved off), everything and everyone I looked at had a clock on them. For instance, I'd look at my grandkids and wonder if I'd see them grow up. I looked at my husband and wondered if I'd make it to retirement with him. Those thoughts threatened to oppress my spirit.

However, as I released my fears and future to God, He anointed me with His hope and assurance that He would walk every step with me, come what may. After all the many blessings He'd given me, did I think He couldn't take care of my family if I weren't here? Of course He could handle it.

My joy has been in place since. Does that mean I'm happy about the cancer? No, I can't say that I am. Do I think God can use it for good? Most definitely. Is my heart full of cheer? You bet it is! I love my life with my family and friends, but the thing is, it only gets better from here. One day I will be with my Lord for all eternity. The knowledge of where I am and where I'm going gives my heart a continual feast.

The next time you feel grumpy, remember that God is there, ready to help you through whatever struggle you're facing. Sorry to break it to you, but although chocolate is good, it's just not enough. ✳ *Diann*

Today's Prayer

Father, You amaze me beyond words. Thank You for
a deep, abiding joy that strengthens and reminds me that
through the struggles of life, the raging hormones,
and the fragile emotions, You are all I need.

Boggled Minds

Set your minds on things above, not on earthly things.

COLOSSIANS 3:2

Sometimes it seems as though clutter begets clutter—whether it's a piece of paper I lay on a table or a thought that muddles my mind. There are so many examples of clutter, it's not possible to mention all of them... so I'll start with my dining room table. We seldom use it for its intended purpose, and it's become a catchall for stuff we're not sure what to do with. On my way to my bedroom, sometimes I plop something on the table with the intention of handling it later—but later may be a day from now or even the next time I dust, which isn't all that often anymore. It starts with one small sheet of paper, and by day's end, like a magnet, it has attracted what seems like a mountain of paperwork.

Then there's the mental clutter that bogs me down so much I don't know where to begin. It wakes me up some mornings, creating a sense of panic that I'll never get through what needs to be done. And it keeps me awake at night as I worry about how I can accomplish all I need to do. The more I think about my concerns, the more scrambled they become, until I have a huge mess in my mind that has me tossing and turning all night... and snapping at people who slow me down during the day.

So what happens if we don't deal with any of that mess—from the physical clutter to the mental bog? Oh, there are some things you should handle, or you'll have a bigger problem later. If there's a bill involved, you'd better pay it. Some big decisions such as buying a new house or trading a car need careful consideration. Or if it's an invitation from someone you care about, you need to RSVP. If your child needs you, be there. And instead of letting your daily concerns clutter your mind or your dining room table, handle them once so you can file them away.

Other than those few things, not much else is important enough to clutter our lives. Our focus should be on God and His plan for us. Worry never serves any purpose, except to take our eyes, hearts, and minds off Him.

Every thought that enters our minds needs to be filtered by our faith in Jesus and what He's called us to do. Instead of shuffling along with too much clutter that is ultimately meaningless, focus on the big picture. It's impossible to truly put Jesus first in your life and still worry about insignificant things. ✳ Debby

Today's Prayer

Lord Jesus, fill me with the focus I need to keep
thinking about heavenly matters rather than insignificant
earthly things. I pray that my life on earth will fulfill
the purpose You have for my existence. Amen.

Clueless Comfort 101

All of you, live in harmony with one another; be sympathetic,
love as brothers, be compassionate and humble.

1 PETER 3:8

*D*on't get me wrong here—I'm not claiming to have figured out all the answers after twenty-three years on this side of salvation. But I'm better than I used to be.

Years ago, when I was taking my first stumbling baby steps in my walk with Jesus, I loved hanging out with one of my more eccentric friends. Gina was a good old gal from North Dakota. She was feminine but tough; she was flirtatious but independent; and she always spoke her mind. In fact, sometimes she embarrassed the living daylights out of me with her blunt comments to me and others. But Gina always made me laugh, and she had a 24-karat-gold heart, which was one of the things I loved most about her. Certainly not a woman of means, she was nonetheless generous with what she had, including her affection. She cared far more about others than about herself.

So it was with confusion that I listened to her complaints one day, when she faced a number of significant disappointments in her life. We stood in her apartment, and I listened as she unloaded the list of events that had brought her down. She started to cry as she spoke. I looked at my normally strong, upbeat friend with what I assumed she recognized as concern. I wanted to be there for her as a good friend and as a Christian. I tried to think of what I was going to say to make her feel better and hopeful.

Finally, she stopped talking, heaved a sigh of exasperation, and spoke to me as if I were frustratingly clueless (which I was). "Oh, *Trish*! Will you just give me a *hug*?"

I blinked stupidly a few times and then stepped forward and hugged the poor girl. That's all she wanted from me. That's why she was kvetching about her lot in life. She needed nothing more than a hug. A shoulder to cry on. No pithy comments, just a physical demonstration that someone cared. I was so used to watching Gina show sympathy to others (and to me), I'd lost sight of the fact that she probably needed someone to return the favor on occasion.

I remember that moment whenever someone chooses me as their sounding board. They're not always asking for a solution. Yes, I've hugged a few people who rebuffed the gesture, which was a little awkward. But, hey, that's where the "humble" part of Peter's verse comes in, right? ✻ Trish

Today's Prayer

Lord Jesus, please keep me alert today to the needs of others. Help me to discern if there is something I can do to bring harmony to a situation, to feel and show sympathy where needed, to love my sisters and brothers, and to show the compassion and humility You demonstrated so long ago. Amen.

Weighting

Wait for the LORD; be strong and take heart and wait for the LORD.

PSALM 27:14

I sent a quick email to a friend: "I haven't heard from you in ages. What are you up to?"

Her reply came the next day. "Same as always. Just weighting."

Weighting? Was she being cryptic? I had to pick up the phone and find out. When I pointed out the incorrect spelling in Kelly's email, it turned out (at least in her mind) to be an honest mistake. Her story convinced me, however, that it may have been a bit Freudian.

For almost a year, Kelly played the role of the silent brokenhearted wife, knowing full well that the man she'd married now had another woman in his life. Then one afternoon, she returned from the office to find her home devoid of every last trace of her husband of thirteen years. Jason had taken his clothes, electronics, stacks of opened mail, the framed photos of his parents, even the blue toothbrush that stood next to Kelly's red one. On the kitchen counter was a note scribbled on the back of a takeout menu. "I can't do this anymore. Sorry."

When I reached her that day, I found Kelly curled up in a ball on the bedroom floor, crying like a baby. An hour later, she was still sobbing and I was on the floor too, my arms around my friend, struggling to find some speck of comfort to offer her. So when she later told me that her future plans revolved around waiting for Jason to come to his senses and return to her, I was the one who wanted to cry.

But wait Kelly did. Week after week, month after month, she waited, praying every day that God would reward her with the return of her husband. The misspelling in her email reminded me what a heavy burden she'd been carrying. "Waiting on the Lord" had been an enormous "weight" on Kelly. She sounded exhausted, weary from the battle, but not so weary that she might give up.

"I still believe Jason will come home," she told me. "I know God put us together for a reason. Until He changes my heart, I have no choice. I'm waiting on the Lord."

Despite my own lack of faith in Jason's redemption, I really admire my friend for hanging on the way that she has. Her own devotion to the promises of God inspire me to question how many times in my life I may have missed out on something because I didn't have the fortitude to hang on and see how the Lord might turn the situation around. ✳ *Sandie*

Today's Prayer

Father, I ask for Your forgiveness for all the times that
I've dropped the ball too soon or discouraged someone else
who had been believing in something that seemed preposter-
ous to me. Let me act as an encourager and uplifter rather than
someone who deflates or tears down with my unbelief. Amen.

Mirror, Mirror on the Wall

Therefore we do not lose heart. Though outwardly we are wasting away,
yet inwardly we are being renewed day by day.

2 CORINTHIANS 4:16

When I look in the mirror, the following Scripture almost always comes to mind: "Charm is deceptive, and beauty is fleeting; but a woman who fears the LORD is to be praised" (Proverbs 31:30). Now why do I hear that in my head when I look in the mirror?

It's a rhetorical question, just so you know.

My daughter is a photographer. When she takes a picture of me, she fixes it. You know, she uses all her fancy know-how to ease the wrinkles and give me a flawless complexion. She thickens my hair and whitens my teeth. In short, when all is said and done, the picture doesn't look like me at all. And I'm okay with that.

Then I take a look in my mirror, and reality hits. The real me in living Technicolor. And if I really want to punish myself, I pick up the mirror that magnifies a hundred times. That one always drives me to chocolate.

Just once I would like for my mirror to lie to me.

So I buy into all the creams, foundations, age-spot reducers—anything short of cosmetic surgery (there's just something very frightening about having a knife near my face; I grow wrinkles just thinking about it)—in hopes of keeping my grandma's age-worn face from looking back at me in the mirror.

The bottom line? I'm growing older. So what? There are worse things, right? Say, like root canals, espionage torture, and a chocolate strike.

My body may be wasting away, but the more time I spend with the Lord, the more my inner self is being renewed. That's why there are so many sweet little grandmas spreading joy in our world—they've spent plenty of time in His presence.

Now, don't get me wrong. I think it's perfectly fine to look our best. After all, we represent Jesus, and we want to look and be our best for His glory. So go ahead and use your creams or whatever makes you feel better about yourself. Just remember, the world is all about making money, so they try to get you to buy those things to fill their pockets. I finally came to the conclusion that there's not enough cold cream on the face of this earth to get rid of all my wrinkles. I buy some, yes, but I'm learning self-control. I don't go out and buy the next thing that comes out on the market. In short, I'm learning to be at peace with who I am at this age. Besides, there is comfort in knowing that true beauty shines from the inside out.

So spend more time with Jesus. Your face will thank you, and so will everyone in your corner of the world. ✳ *Diann*

Today's Prayer

Father, help me to reflect Your beauty today
and every day. In Jesus' name, amen.

So Very Righteous!

Gray hair is a crown of splendor; it is attained by a righteous life.

PROVERBS 16:31

Let's face it, gray hair doesn't feel all that glorious. In fact, "restoring" our natural color from gray is a billion-dollar industry. How many natural blonds do you think actually exist? We are inundated daily with a shallow image of the perfect woman. She has a Pilates figure. She has long, lustrous hair without extensions, and her wrinkles have been erased by a toxic filler.

In a world obsessed with beauty, we can lose sight of the fact that God tells us beauty is fleeting; as the outside is crumbling, the inside is becoming more beautiful. What's so wonderful about this verse is that it reminds us that although we as humans may focus on the exterior, God is concerned with renewing our souls each day, and life should cost us something. If we remain untouched by living, have we actually experienced life?

One of my magazines arrived with two separate stories. One was about a "real housewife" who, at 47, looks like she's 27. Her skin is dewy and taut. Her complexion shows no visible signs of aging. Her blond hair appears bouncy and brilliant. On the very next page was the story of a woman who looks about 65 but is also 47. She wears long, straggly gray hair. Her clothes are ill-fitting, and her hands are wrinkled and covered with age spots. She has lived her entire life in a coal miner's realm and recently lost her husband in an underground explosion.

The irony of these two women, these two stories just one page apart, was not lost on me. One of them was being held up as a model of beauty for her age; the other, as a victim of a rough life. Like a stretched wineskin, the latter had used herself to the point of strain, while the first probably had a full-time staff helping her to look so good.

In heaven, we won't have a staff. We won't need one. God will not judge us by how long we let our roots grow out. He will not ask us about that extra ten pounds of baby fat we carry.

Should we give up vanity altogether? Probably not. Our spouses/children/friends might object, since we do live in society. Do we really want the church to be a standout section of Quasimodos? Maybe not. However, wouldn't it be great if our soul "grew out" and we noticed that first?

"God, I need a touch-up! Come and fill me up!" ✳ Kristin

Today's Prayer

Dear Jesus, thank You for creating me as You did.
I pray today that I would think as much about my soul
as I do about my appearance. Help me to be a woman of
substance today and honor You in the time I spend
on me versus the time I spend with You. Amen.

Shaking in My Boots

*"The fear of the LORD is the beginning of wisdom,
and knowledge of the Holy One is understanding."*

PROVERBS 9:10

When my older daughter, Alison, was not quite three years old, we took a chance and brought her into the church sanctuary. Rather than put her in the nursery or sit in the back, we sat in the second pew from the front. She was well-behaved, and it was the only pew with enough room for us to spread out with my "mommy bag," my husband, Alison, and my nearly-nine-months-pregnant body. That turned out to be one of the most interesting and educational church services we ever attended—one I'll never forget.

Our church was designed with the pews set in a semicircle around the pulpit, where our larger-than-life pastor, with his full beard, piercing eyes, and booming voice, could pace yet stay close to his congregation. He made eye contact with everyone in front of him, so it seemed as though he spoke to each person individually. I noticed that each time he came toward us, Alison would suddenly stiffen. Her mouth would open, and her eyes would widen. I didn't understand what was going on with her until she finally whispered, "Mommy, here comes God." Then she gripped my hand and held on tight until the pastor paced back to the other side of the pulpit.

It took every ounce of self-restraint not to laugh or even smile. I leaned over and whispered back, "Honey, he's not God. He's our pastor who preaches God's Word."

Alison's forehead crinkled as she glanced at Pastor Robinson. She tilted her head and looked at me. "How do you know He's not God?"

It's difficult to explain this to a toddler, but after church, my husband and I did the best we could by explaining that the pastor was a man who was passionate about his faith and was called by God to tell the congregation about His Word. After she was satisfied with our answers, she went to her room to play. Wally and I looked at each other and sighed. Finally he said, "At least she knows the importance of reverence when it comes to the Lord."

We still tease Alison about that day, but my husband had a valid point. Our daughter was in awe of God. Although her image of Him had been placed on a mortal man, she had the innate sense that He wasn't one of us. He's much bigger and greater than we'll ever be, and that is the beginning of the understanding we have through total admiration and awe of our Creator. Whenever I start to get full of myself, I remind myself of our talk with Alison. ✳ *Debby*

Today's Prayer

Dear Jesus, I am in awe of Your holiness. Please fill me
with the desire to stay close to You, and may I follow
You as a walking witness of Your Word. Amen.

Hair Today, Gone...Today

"Who of you by worrying can add a single hour to his life?"

MATTHEW 6:27

My ex-husband and I managed to become comfortable around each other shortly after we parted. A hairdresser, he still cut and colored my hair for me—it was an adventure for both of us. The short time during which we were married and for years afterward, we had fun with my hair, changing its cut and color every few months.

The last time he laid a finger on my locks, though, it merely needed trimming. At the time, I was a bleached blond and wore it in a deliberately tousled 'do nearly down to my shoulders. I loved it. He was just about finished with the trim and had even blown it dry when he stood behind me, studied the results in the mirror, suddenly grabbed the entire right side of my hair, and cut off the handful in one fell swoop. Apparently he had decided an asymmetrical look might be fun.

I couldn't have broken into tears any faster if he had hit me with a brick. We all know how long it takes to grow out hair, and now I hardly had any hair where I'd had quite a lot only moments before. I'm a pale gal, so on the bleached-out, buzz-cut side, I actually looked...bald. Once I got hold of my emotions and all sharp objects had been moved out of my reach, my ex cut the other side—really, what else could I do but let him? And I had him color my hair dark so I'd at least look like I actually *had* hair.

It was a horrid look for me. I was scary. I looked like a puffy, punky Cruella de Vil without the trademark white streak. I didn't make that observation to him—believe me, I wasn't about to give him any other ideas.

I stressed about being seen in public—for months. I had to learn to let it go. For someone as vain as I was then, that took effort. But what if I had worried every day of that awful growing-out period? Would my hair have grown back any faster? No.

So it is with worrying about adversities (or potential adversities) in life—about whether matters will work out as we think they should. Whether our fears come to fruition or don't, whether we get what we want or we don't, will worrying have *any* effect on the outcome of anything? Worrying didn't add a single centimeter to my hair. Will it add a single hour to your life?

God knows what's going on. Trust Him! ✳ *Trish*

Today's Prayer

Lord, when I start to worry, as I inevitably do, please
touch my heart and remind me that You are in control.
Help me to relax in Your plan and wait for life to
unfold as only You know best. Amen.

Here Is Our King

*"But you are a forgiving God, gracious and compassionate,
slow to anger and abounding in love. Therefore you did not desert them...."*

NEHEMIAH 9:17

David Crowder, my favorite worship singer, wrote a song called "Here Is Our King." In it, he likens God to an ocean's tide. I love the passion and feeling of this song, but the visual is so immense and powerful. God keeps coming back. He's as dependable as the ocean's waves. Sometimes the tide goes out. There is more sand and the ocean feels further away, leaving one on the dry sand to wonder if it's not coming back this time—but its power and dependability can be counted upon. Like our majestic God.

As a writer, one faces a lot of rejection, and it's important to be grounded in what you're doing—to know *why* you're doing it. First, there is the constant rejection of trying to get something published. Most writers could wallpaper their entire office with rejection letters.

Second, there's the rejection that editing brings. Though ultimately this will make your book better and ready for the real world, it's still difficult to see all those red markings on a manuscript. No easier than it was in school.

Finally, there is the book's entry into the world and the worst of the rejection. Now it's public, posted on websites. The rejection may read something like, "I don't know how this woman can call herself a Christian! A real Christian would never write this!"

During those times, it feels like the tide—like God our Comforter is so far away, that we are alone. This time, the tide is going to stay out; we just know it. But then...God comes rolling back in, with drops of encouragement and a sign that we are not forgotten. God is so faithful. He will not forget to return.

When we don't deserve it.

When we reject Him as often as Israel did.

When we dethrone Him to be our own god or to worship some ridiculous idol.

If you grew up in a household where parents weren't slow to anger, be reminded of God's gracious heart and of His love, which surpasses anything we will know on this earth. If you're a parent, think of your own child and how many times you would return for him or her. Now add supernatural love and miraculous abilities, and you will know—God is coming back for you, because you are worth it. He created you to be you. Maybe you're not the perfect Christian by the world's standards, but you are the perfect child to Him, and He's the perfect parent.

Like a wave, His love will overwhelm and encompass you. ✳ *Kristin*

Today's Prayer

Dear Jesus, thank You for showing yourself in
the beauty of nature and the resonance of music within my
heart. Help me to see Your great love all around me today.
Let it encompass and surround me. Amen.

Standing in the Storm

A thousand may fall at your side, ten thousand at your right hand,
but it will not come near you.

PSALM 91:7

The inner workings of Corporate America are most definitely not for the faint of heart. Although I'm grateful beyond measure for my day job as an editor, there are so many things about working for a worldwide corporation that rattle the nerves in ways that operating one's own small public relations firm did not.

One of those things is corporate performance. Business decisions must be made based on the whole bucket, not on the individual splashes of water that fill it; and so when economic difficulties come along, everyone hunkers down and waits for the fallout to see how it might unexpectedly affect them.

Rumblings about layoffs and budget cuts had been echoing for weeks. One morning, as we all fetched our coffee and chatted about our weekends as we set about starting the day, the fallout began. One of my favorite coworkers was summoned to human resources, and an hour later, he was clearing out his desk. Then I signed on to the conference bridge for a meeting, and one of the key players failed to show up. Later that day, I was told she'd been let go.

Although my heart wept for them, I couldn't stop my mind from going inward. What if I was next? What would I do without my job? While most everyone else at least had the second income of a spouse to rely upon, I had nothing more than the small, sporadic stipends of a freelance author. My savings might cover a couple of months, but beyond that, what would I do?

Between meetings, I went into a stall in the ladies' room and began to pray. I prayed for my friends who had been laid off, and for their families.

I told the Lord that I knew He would take care of me no matter what occurred; then I took a breath and asked Him to spare me and the rest of the folks around me anyway.

The following week, a list was released to us, naming all our peers who were no longer employed by the company. It was a long list, consisting of very familiar names, but not one person on my immediate team appeared on it. The next day, while spending time in the Word, I came across today's familiar Scripture. I thought of the "thousands" that had fallen at my side, and I cried with gratitude as I realized it had not come near me...because of the Lord's good grace. ✳ *Sandie*

Today's Prayer

Lord, experience tells me that I won't always be spared.
There are going to be challenges in life that will affect me in
significant ways. But thank You for the grace that often shields
me when I reach out for You—and for the assurance that
You will be with me in the other times too. Amen.

You Want Me to Do What? When?

*Each of you should look not only to your own interests,
but also to the interests of others.*

PHILIPPIANS 2:4

$\mathcal{S}$adly, that's usually my response when God asks me to do something I don't want to do.

I love people. I really do. But when it comes to making food, calling people, or helping in some way, I come up with a million excuses for why I can't do it. "I'm not a good cook." "I shouldn't call and bother them; they might be sleeping." "If I go to their home, what will I say?"

Moses has nothin' on me.

For me, it seems to be more of an inferiority complex than an uncaring attitude, but it's one I have to overcome just the same.

Now, granted, there are times I don't understand why I should do something. Case in point: a long time ago, I felt a gentle nudge in my spirit to give a lady a ham. It made no sense to me, but I did it just the same. Her response? "I don't know why you gave me this, but thanks."

Years later, when I shared the story with another friend, she said, "Maybe God wanted you to give her a *hand* and you thought He said *ham*."

Oh, well. I was obedient and she got a ham. It was a win-win situation.

It helps to remember that God sees the whole picture. In obedience, we trust that God will use our efforts for His glory.

My neighbors are excellent examples of people who serve others. They both were teachers who retired a couple of years ago. Since that time, we have seen them travel for missions, help others with remodeling, prepare meals, make phone calls, plan visits—you name it, they've done it. It doesn't matter if it's backbreaking work or as simple as picking up a phone, they serve without hesitation.

They are my heroes.

It's true enough that serving doesn't come easily to everyone, but the fact of the matter is, we're all called to look to the interests of others. So I've tried to start making a list each morning (yes, I'm one of those) to help me remember to do something for someone during the day I'm given. (You do realize every day is a gift, right?)

How do you remember to reach out to others? Does it come naturally to you? Do you make a list of some kind? Do you allow your day to plan itself and reach out only if someone calls you with a need?

I'm not saying there is any right or wrong way. The important thing is that we do it. Is there someone right now who needs you? ✳ *Diann*

Today's Prayer

Father, as I go about my day today, help me to look to
the interests of others whom You bring to mind.

Don't Get Wise,
Bubble Eyes

Do not be wise in your own eyes; fear the LORD and shun evil.

PROVERBS 3:7

I'll never forget my college semester exams. Every time they rolled around, I invested in a jar of instant coffee, pulled out all my notes from the class lectures, and locked myself in my dorm room, resisting the temptation to go hang out with friends who didn't intend to return the next semester. I needed to study so I could make good enough grades to come back and do it all over again until I graduated. I spent hours going through my notes, trying to figure out what might be on the exams. As I memorized facts, I gained knowledge—some that would slip away after the exam and some that might stick in my head. After the exams were over, I awaited (sometimes eagerly, but often with dread) my final grade in each class. I took classes year-round, so I managed to graduate in a little more than three years. How smart was that?

After successfully completing the requirements of my degree, it didn't take long to discover the difference between knowledge and wisdom. In job after job, I found that the courses I took were abstract and not always applicable in the real world. And I also learned that college hadn't prepared me for everything life threw at me. What a blow to my self-inflated ego. I had the knowledge from years of studies but not the wisdom to apply it. Fortunately, I'd gone to church off and on throughout college. During my last semester and my internship, I met a retired pastor and started attending church with his family. Through them, I learned the difference between God's wisdom and my own. How humbling!

I don't know where the saying "Don't get wise, bubble eyes" came from, but I remember hearing it—and, yes, I'll admit saying it a few times—quite a bit during the seventies. I don't think the biblical implications of it crossed our minds back then, but think about it. When we rely on our own limited wisdom without filtering it through our Christian worldview, we're generally wrong. Trusting in our own wisdom is like trying to swim across an ocean without a lifeboat. There are so many things we don't know and can't possibly ever know.

Most people equate wisdom with knowledge...and in our human perspective, that's accurate. However, I can research and study for days, months, or years to gain knowledge, yet I may still not have much more wisdom. God's wisdom is all-encompassing; ours is limited as it is sifted through our wants, needs, and personal experiences. ✳ *Debby*

Today's Prayer

Father in heaven, thank You for Your mercy and
forgiveness for the times I think I'm wiser than I really am.
As I go through each day, grant me the wisdom to rely
on Your Word over my own knowledge. Amen.

Change Is Good

Jesus Christ is the same yesterday and today and forever.

HEBREWS 13:8

ou know, I've been thinking," my sister said one day. "When I was in my twenties, I knew I had behaved like an idiot in my teens."

I had to agree with her there. We both had.

"And then, in my thirties, I looked back on my twenties. I made some horrible decisions in my twenties. Horrible! So I was pretty much an idiot in my twenties too." She laughed and shook her head about her naïveté.

I wasn't sure I liked where this conversation was going.

"I thought I had it all going on by the time I was thirty," she said. "But now, in my forties, I can see that I didn't know what I was doing in my thirties either. So I was kind of an idiot then, no matter what I thought at the time."

She shrugged and pushed her lips out, a world-weary heaviness to her eyelids. "It's taken me all this time to figure it out. Maybe I'm just an idiot."

Of course, she exaggerated. She had done plenty of growing and learning, just as we all do. But I understood her point. We usually don't go through life thinking we're clueless or deliberately making bad decisions—turning left when we really should be turning right or saying yes when, in hindsight, a big fat *no* was so obviously the wiser answer. But part of changing and growing is recognizing your mistakes of the past, determining to do better in the present, and taking for granted you'll look back in the future and adjust for where you went right or wrong.

For us, change is good.

But what utter chaos life would be if Jesus were like we are. If His life goals in His thirties changed as a result of what He experienced at the hands of man...if He retracted His promise to be with us always, "to the very end of the age," when it was clear how much of our lives we would squander while doing stupid or sinful things.

Of course, His eternal stability doesn't mean He's a cardboard cutout. He's not devoid of humor, appreciation, sorrow, or care over how we live our lives. But we can't surprise Him with our behavior. He knew about every facet of our behavior before He chose to die for us. So He'll never desert us. He'll always love us. His requirement of us will always be the same: to accept His love and the sacrifice He made for us. That has never changed, and it never will. ✳ *Trish*

Today's Prayer

Precious Lord Jesus, thank You for loving me and
for making the ultimate sacrifice for me. I understand You knew
my every sin and failing—even those I haven't yet committed—
when You bought my redemption. Thank You that Your
love for me will never change. Amen.

Fine by Me

All a man's ways seem right to him, but the LORD weighs the heart.

PROVERBS 21:2

I love to be right. In a gleeful, in-your-face kind of way. I'm not proud of it, but I have to admit this dark part of my personality. Worse yet, I'm a trivia buff, so I'm right a good part of the time.

Do you despise me yet?

I picked up this little habit (one might say *sin nature*) from my father. He loves to be right as well. The problem is, we never agree on anything, and while our arguments have led us to many an Internet check as we search for the facts, ultimately neither of us is inclined to change our opinions. We generally stick to our own belief system and walk away satisfied. The rest of the dinner table may be left fighting indigestion, but my father and I are fulfilled, each feeling a sense of rightness.

The thing about this kind of "rightness" is that, by its very nature, it stirs up dissension, which God hates. Then, if you add the whole "honor thy father and mother" idea, I'm on very shaky ground. Still, I know these arguments stir my father's heart in a good-for-his-digestion kind of way. It keeps us both developing more brain cells.

This is why I love Proverbs 21:2. *God looks at the heart.* He knows my motives. He knows how much I love my earthly father and want to see him in the kingdom with me and his grandchildren. God also knows that my father, being Italian and all, loves a good argument.

To me, today's Scripture is a daily-check verse. Is my heart in the right place? Am I doing this in love or because "God says so"? Am I beating someone over the head with my views sans love?

The story of Mary and Martha is the perfect biblical showcase of how God looks at the heart (see Luke 10:38–41). Martha is distracted by the preparations, while Mary sits at Jesus's feet and listens. Martha tattles, "Lord, don't you care that my sister has left me to do all the work by myself?"

Jesus replies, "Martha, Martha, you are worried and upset about many things, but only one thing is needed. Mary has chosen what is better, and it will not be taken away from her."

Oh, snap! Martha's motives were not from a place of love. They focused on duty. How easy it can be to assume that someone is acting in love when they are, in fact, wanting to be noticed for their efforts. Sometimes the love comes after an event, like when we volunteer for our church nursery and grow to love the children. The point is that we must constantly search our hearts and check our motives.

Being right isn't always what it appears to be on the surface. ✳ *Kristin*

Today's Prayer

Dear heavenly Father, hold my motives pure in my heart. Help me to do Your will here on earth today out of a genuine love for You and a desire to please You and do the right thing. Amen.

unHappy Anniversary

*"You will forget the shame of your youth and remember
no more the reproach of your widowhood. For your Maker
is your husband—the LORD Almighty is his name."*

ISAIAH 54:4–5

Coop and Lynette had been married for thirty years. Despite their silver hair and matching crow's feet, one might have suspected they'd just met after five minutes in their presence. Coop pulled out her chair and brought her roses at least once each month, and he lit up the whole place the instant Lynette floated through any doorway toward him.

They didn't have a lot of money, but they managed to put a little away all year toward the standing anniversary tradition they'd developed. Dressed to the tens in their ballroom-best, after an elegant dinner at one of the city's finest restaurants, Coop took Lynette dancing. She said that waltzing with her husband never failed to bring visions of fairy tales and happily-ever-afters.

Coop had been called to Phoenix just before their thirty-first anniversary, but he called Lynette from the road and said he would be home in plenty of time to shower and change so that they could make their seven p.m. dinner reservation. By six o'clock, Lynette put the finishing touches on her hair, sprayed it into place, and sat down in the chair by the window. She dropped a few items into her evening bag while she watched for Coop's arrival.

At seven, she called Coop's friend in Phoenix; at 7:30, her heart began to race; by 8:30, she twisted the ribbon on her elegant green dress as she dialed the state police. By eleven o'clock that night, Lynette recounted later, she realized that her life was over. Coop had been killed in a head-on collision while his wife waited for him to take her dancing.

A year passed before the realization set in and two years until her first thought every morning didn't flash to Coop. After four years, we happened across each other's paths at the dry cleaner and went to a nearby café for tea. I asked the vibrant, smiling woman across from me how she'd managed.

"Coop did everything for me," she said before glancing up at me with an intent smile. "I was completely out of my element without him; I was terrified. But what I came to realize is that Coop was only on loan to me. My true Husband, the One with me when I came into this world and the One with me when I eventually leave it, never departs from me. Jesus is my True Companion."

Lynette's assurance and solid faith pricked me in that moment with the reminder that no matter how connected we are to the people around us, those people are only on loan to us. Our Maker, Savior, Husband, Provider, and Healer come in one consistent, dependable, divorce-free partner. ✳ *Sandie*

Today's Prayer

Lord, thank You so much for your steadfast love.
Whether I am married, single, or somewhere in between,
You are my Husband, and I have nothing to fear. Amen.

A Quiet Place

*Then, because so many people were coming and going
that they did not even have a chance to eat, he said to them,
"Come with me by yourselves to a quiet place and get some rest."*

MARK 6:31

Now that I've reached my fifties, I truly understand the meaning of a quiet place. When my kids were young, this place of complete and utter silence was a magical land of which I merely dreamed. Many of you can identify with that. You haven't experienced quiet since 1995.

Life is noisy. Kids, cars, barking dogs, the hustle-and-bustle of life— all noisy. Even in Jesus's day, this was the case. I can imagine the sounds of bleating sheep, people negotiating in the marketplace, camels stirring, the *clip-clop* of donkeys' hooves, mothers warning young children to stay close, children squealing and laughing, the *thump* of sandals upon hard ground.

Crowds followed Jesus and his disciples. Scores of people crushed them on every side, eager to hear the Good News. The people had needs. Some were curious. Some were hungry for Truth. Some were spies. No doubt the disciples were emotionally drained and physically spent.

Jesus called them to a quiet place for rest.

We have a small courtyard in front of our house that I have filled with plants and flowers that burst with blooms in May. A wooden bench is nestled within this garden sanctuary, and I love to take my journal and sit out there...in the quiet. Well, it's not exactly quiet. Nature plays a symphony in the mornings, which I love. I'm surrounded by the sound of jubilant birds announcing the start of a new day. The sun eagerly bids me a happy hello, while my plants shine with the polish of morning. I call it my retreat. My getaway. *My quiet place.* It's where I go to talk with my

Lord and praise Him for the gift of a new day. To relish the quiet, gentle moments with Him before the demands of the day take over.

Do you have such a place?

Sometimes we have to get creative. For busy moms, a quiet place may consist of a bathroom break, an early morning closet appointment, a cup of tea at the table during nap time.

But here's something else I've learned. Even in the chaos of a busy day, I can retreat to my quiet place, my inner soul, where no one else goes but God and me. I can share a whispered moment of conversation with my Lord, no matter where I am at the time, and calm immediately drifts through my spirit like an inner tube on a lazy river.

Quiet moments are waiting in unexpected corners, rooms, and heart chambers. You need only to look for them, long for them, and go to them. Meet Him in the quiet places of your heart. It will make all the difference in your day. ✳ *Diann*

Today's Prayer

Thank You for always meeting me in my quiet place.

Forever Young

Do not cast me away when I am old;
do not forsake me when my strength is gone.

PSALM 71:9

ot young chicks are in high demand in this world; shriveled-up old prunes are not. The question is, who gets to decide at what point the hot chick is all dried-up and ready to be cast aside? Our kids? Our grandkids? Um...I don't think so. At least not now...maybe never.

I remember thinking in my late teens and early twenties that anyone over thirty was old. Back in the day (never mind the year), once a woman reached the big three-oh, she either started wearing double-knits and orthotics or she lied about her age.

Fortunately, things have changed and the old-age line has shifted. Cosmetic companies began producing beauty products to smooth out our wrinkles and erase age spots, making fifty the new thirty. Our kids grew up with hip moms who looked like they could be older sisters—much to the kids' dismay. We started working out and staying in shape. We have cool haircuts that cost more than dinner out for a family of four. Our hair color is whatever we want it to be, and we don't mind changing it to the hue du jour. There's no need to get old, even when we're ready for the retirement home. From what I hear, there's some serious partying going on in those places these days.

I have two daughters who are both in their twenties. One is a single, educated, career woman, and the other is a married, educated mommy. Yeah, that makes me a grandmother, but, hey, we haven't determined where that old-age line is yet—although my children might look at it differently. When my daughters were little, they thought I was smart. At some point in the preteen years, I became a feebleminded meddler and invisible when it was convenient. Then as they blossomed into adults, the most amazing thing happened: I suddenly got smart again. Now I'm grateful that my daughters and I have a warm, loving relationship based on mutual respect. I can't imagine them or my husband turning me away as I grow old and wrinkled.

As I think about this verse, "Do not cast me away when I am old...," I also consider myself fortunate that as a believer, I never have to worry about God getting tired of me or seeing me as less worthy of His love at any point in my life, no matter how old I get. Old age may steal my taut, firm skin and replace it with a saggy, baggy hide, but I know the Lord sees beauty in His creation. ✳ *Debby*

Today's Prayer

Lord, thank You for the assurance of Your love
even as the years pile on top of each other and add
texture to the skin. Let us see the wisdom in Your
plan and help us grow closer to You. Amen.

The Right Words at the Right Time

A man finds joy in giving an apt reply—and how good is a timely word!

PROVERBS 15:23

Years ago, at a family gathering, we had so many people attending the meal that many of us sat away from the table with our plates in our laps. My older brother, dressed in his finest, sat on the rug cross-legged, cradling his plate with his legs. Without warning, his plate flipped like a Tiddlywink, and his entire meal—roast beef, gravy, potatoes, gravy, peas, *did I say gravy?*—poured swiftly into his lap.

Everyone around him grabbed their plates and moved out of the way as if his food were explosive. He sat in shock, staring at his lap.

My mother, however, said, "Boy, are *you* lucky."

Now, I'm sure what my mother meant was something like, "Boy, are you lucky your food had cooled somewhat; otherwise, you would have burned yourself something fierce." Or, "Boy, are you lucky your food didn't spill all over the Persian rug. It will cost far less to dry-clean your suit than to clean or replace that rug." Or, "Boy, are you lucky you're not on a date, because you look pretty ridiculous right now."

But the timing and wording of Mom's comment prompted my brother to laugh incredulously and point to the mess in his lap. "You call *this* lucky?"

We've all had times when we meant well but chose the wrong words or spoke in an untimely manner: a compliment to one person insulted another; an offhanded attempt at humor turned out to be grossly inappropriate; a comment to make a point shouldn't have been made at that particular moment.

And then there are those wonderful experiences when the Lord uses our words to give comfort, to bring joy, to verify one of His truths, or to draw someone closer to Him. Sometimes we don't even realize it's happening. Once I made an off-the-cuff comment to a seeker and later learned it was instrumental in her coming to Christ. I definitely "[found] joy in giving an apt reply."

We needn't be poets, either. Years ago, a Christian friend spoke to me about Jesus. All I remember today is how she inhaled as if smelling a beautiful aroma before saying, "He's just so...*wonderful.*"

As Christians we represent Jesus, so it makes sense to pray that He'll bless us with the right words at the right time, especially if what we say might open someone's heart to Him. ✳ *Trish*

Today's Prayer

Dearest Lord, it's such a privilege to be used by You, to say
something You want us to say to a person in need, in pain, in joy,
or in search of You. I ask that You use me that way often...and
that You help me to keep my mind open to Your guidance and
Your words. Please give me discerning judgment to speak
Your words when they will do the most good. Amen.

Eat and Be Merry

"Blessed are you who hunger now, for you will be satisfied.
Blessed are you who weep now, for you will laugh."

LUKE 6:21

Have you ever been in a place where you thought you'd never laugh again? Sometimes the burdens of life can be so daunting, it's hard to see the way out, much less have a giggle during the valley. And hunger? I know people who have been on a diet for their entire lives, and they don't ever seem satisfied. So when I see God's promises written out the way they are in today's verse, seeming so elusive and miraculous, I often question my own sanity and ponder the question, "Does God mean in this lifetime?"

When my kids were young, I used to scrapbook. Now that they're older, I'm so busy driving them around, I never have time to document the occasions—but the finished books have reminded me that what was once so painful is now a great source of laughter. Maybe that's what God means: that we'll view life differently from another vantage point.

When I had four children under six years of age, I did not live in the present much—I *survived*. I barked orders and expected compliance, though sometimes more explanation was actually necessary. One Easter, my church had an outdoor Good Friday service, complete with communion. I'd been raised Catholic, where children didn't get to take communion until they'd gone through a series of classes and understood the depth of the encounter. Why I thought my boys (aged two, four, and five) would understand this, I'm not sure. They were all whining for dinner, but my husband and I said to the boys, "We're going to take communion and come back to the car, and we'll go eat."

They all nodded. We hurried to the front of the line so that we could leave and get the kids fed—it was late for them. We ripped off our pieces of communion bread and headed to the minivan. When I finally turned around to help them into the van and tell my boys about communion, instead of the great teachable moment I imagined, they stood next to the vehicle with an entire loaf of French bread, and their chipmunk cheeks were round and in motion.

"Did you take the communion bread?" I asked in horror.

"We're not hungry anymore," my oldest said with a happy smile.

My husband arrived, and I pointed out our latest family faux pas. "Should I take it back?"

"Do you think they want it back?" he asked.

I supposed not.

God will bring us joy from the ashes. He will satisfy our hungers and cries even if we're too weak to know what to ask Him for. He understands. ✳ *Kristin*

Today's Prayer

Dear Jesus, give me joy today. Help me to belly laugh
and be grateful for the days You have given me, even though
some are better than others. Make today a good one and help me
to spread laughter and happiness in the moment. If I must wait,
help me to be patient and remember that You have the best
interests for my journey already written. Amen.

Heritage Rights

"No weapon forged against you will prevail, and you will refute every tongue that accuses you. This is the heritage of the servants of the LORD, and this is their vindication from me," declares the LORD.

ISAIAH 54:17

During more than ten years of friendship, Carol became a sort of spiritual mother to me. She taught me so much, not just by sharing her profound knowledge of God's Word and His principles, but also by modeling behavior as my mentor and example.

Carol and her husband were very wealthy, and she told me many times what a mixed blessing that could be. I came to understand the meaning well after her husband passed away and people with dollar signs in their eyes crept out of the woodwork. My friend found herself immersed in turmoil, anxiety, and lawsuits, all while she dealt with her own devastating loss. Javelins of accusation flew at her, lies swirled around her—and much like the labor pains of a pregnant woman, the intensity of each attack increased in severity.

We would sneak away sometimes in the afternoon to one of Carol's favorite spots and order large cups of hazelnut coffee and one warm berry tart with a scoop of ice cream on top, which we split. We cried together and prayed together, and often the afternoon came to a close with the two of us giggling about what the Lord was sure to do in order to bring about vindication.

The war waged against Carol came in sporadic, heated battles. But each time, my friend held fast to the spirit of the same Scripture, claiming the promise of God that it is our very heritage as His children: accusing tongues will be refuted, and weapons formed against us will not prosper.

"I don't know how you do it," I told her one afternoon. "How do you keep going?"

"I have a very sharp sword," she told me, referring to the sword of the spirit, which is the Word of God. "I have the promise that, at the end of this road, I'll be vindicated."

My friend eventually found that vindication, and those attackers insinuating themselves into every fold of her life disappeared. Years passed, and we often spoke of the wonderful final victory.

Carol passed away a couple of years ago, and I've never quite recovered from the loss. I cling vehemently to those things I learned from my dear friend, to the secret conversations and all the giggles we shared. Recently, however, those same enemies that disappeared so long ago have resurfaced, staking a claim to everything they lost the first time around. And every time I pray about my fresh anger and resentment toward them, I am armed with just the right Scripture, the one that fits perfectly in my hand in the form of a sword. ✳ Sandie

Today's Prayer

Lord, may You always be victorious on behalf of Your children,
and may the weapons formed against us never prosper.
Vindication is Yours, and for that I praise Your name! Amen.

Dignity, Really?

She is clothed with strength and dignity;
she can laugh at the days to come.

PROVERBS 31:25

After I was diagnosed with ovarian cancer, the Lord seemed to impress today's Scripture upon my mind. I couldn't imagine why that verse, of all verses, would come to my mind time and again. Later, God seemed to confirm through two other people that it would be *my verse* for the road I was traveling.

I'm writing this four months after my diagnosis, and the verse has served me well—all except for the dignity thing. Maybe it's just me, but I don't feel very dignified without hair. I mean, if I try to imagine myself bald in front of, oh, my favorite singer (Wayne Watson) or my favorite Bible teacher (Beth Moore), I will tell you right here and right now, that "dignity" thing won't be working for me—to say nothing of the no eyebrows/eyelashes thing.

However, to be honest, not having hair has its rewards. I never have to shave my legs. Facial hair is no longer a concern. And it only takes me five minutes to get "my" hair ready for public viewing.

God has given me His strength, for which I am grateful. His joy fills my days, so I have no trouble laughing at the days to come, for which I'm also grateful.

Still, there's that "dignity" word. And please don't get me started about all the prodding, poking, and invasion of privacy I have going on when I'm in the presence of medical personnel. Where is the dignity in that?

Such a little word, but how it had haunted me at night when I stretched on my turban. It followed me into the doctor's office when I draped on a paper-thin gown with more openings than a Broadway play.

So with great frustration, I decided to look up the word in the dictionary. Listen to this; it's so cool. One of the definitions simply said "Worthiness."

Worthiness? I never in a million years would have put those words together—dignity...worthiness? Wow. As I pondered that explanation, the reality of what God's Word was saying to me began to seep into my understanding. Just as I am clothed in His strength, I am clothed in His dignity. In other words, I am wrapped in *His* worthiness, not mine! I can laugh at the days to come because *He* is worthy!

Woo-hooo!

No one wants to be sick, least of all have cancer—but knowing that He is with us every step of our earthly journey, come what may (illness, divorce, financial distress...), and knowing that He clothes us with His strength and His dignity (worthiness), we truly can laugh at the days to come! ✳ *Diann*

Today's Prayer

Dearest Adonai, I'm so thankful that when our hearts
are broken, You are there. When answers aren't enough,
You are there. Thank You for Your strength, dignity, and
joy that covers me today, no matter what the circumstances.

I Could Have
Been Someone

*But I am like an olive tree flourishing in the house of God;
I trust in God's unfailing love for ever and ever.*

P S A L M   5 2 : 8

I could have really been somebody. If I'd gotten that job I applied for right out of college, my life would be totally different. It would have been the perfect position for me to climb the corporate ladder and really make a name for myself.

After getting my degree in Recreational Administration, I assumed I'd be able to march into my favorite theme park corporate office, knock on the human resources door, and be welcomed with open arms. Instead, the expressionless receptionist handed me a paper application, told me to fill it out, and asked which character I wanted to try out for.

Character? Me? I chuckled. No, she didn't understand. I wanted to be *in charge* of the characters. I wanted to plan recreational activities for the guests. After she listened to my explanation, her lips turned upward into a smirk. "Do you want a job at the park or not?" she asked.

Sheepishly, I accepted the application, walked over to one of the tables, and started filling it out. Okay, so I'd start out as a character— probably Grumpy, based on the way I was feeling at the time. But I'd be the best Grumpy they ever had, and they'd see my brilliance. It wouldn't be long before I'd get promoted to the job of my dreams.

After I finished filling out the application, I got up and walked over to the long line that had formed in front of the reception desk. The guy at the head of the line asked if they promoted from within—and if so, what his chances were of getting a better job in a year or so. The receptionist told him it was a possibility but highly unlikely because they used headhunters for permanent positions. My future was beginning to dim, but being the positive person I am, I handed her my application with a forced smile. She took it and said they'd get back to me if they were interested. At that moment, I knew my future wasn't at that theme park.

On my way home, I prayed that the Lord would direct me to a career path that was right for me. I had no idea what else I wanted to do, because after reading about a guy who was an activities director for a major theme park, that was all I ever thought I wanted. No other career appealed to me at the time. But as the years passed, God took control and directed me in the path of His choosing. And I have no doubt that His wisdom put me into the place that is best for me. ✳ *Debby*

Today's Prayer

Thank You, Lord, for reigning over my life.
I have no regretsabout what might have been,
because You know my destiny. Amen.

Talk a Lot, Talk a Little More

Perfume and incense bring joy to the heart, and the pleasantness of one's friend springs from his earnest counsel.

PROVERBS 27:9

Some of my friends are single women. A few are dating again; a few aren't. But the evolution of the dating relationships has been fascinating, and some of our comments could only be comfortably made between friends who trust each other.

"I've decided I like my life the way it is. I love dating Ben, but I like to get home to my own place too."

"I just really want to be married again. I miss taking care of a man."

"I think you're looking for a reason to stop seeing Ed, but he's too nice to break up with."

"I don't really want romance. I'd just like to have a male friend to go out with once in a while."

"I want that last piece of cheesecake."

Obviously, dating isn't our only topic of conversation. We deliberate decisions about our children, our jobs, our health, our plans. We discuss our faith and how the Lord has touched us. We get together and enjoy the occasional meal or movie, but the main point of our gatherings is to talk out life. Women need that. That's how God designed us.

John Gray's *Men Are from Mars, Women Are from Venus* was released in 1992, yet so much of what he wrote still rings true nearly two decades later. I think he hit quite a few nails on the head.

I was married for years before I managed to get occasional time away with girlfriends. I still remember how I came home after the first time, absolutely light-headed with pleasure. Although I enjoyed my family time, I had forgotten how important my friends were. I hadn't talked and laughed so much in ages. It's just different with women than it is with men or kids. And when a woman needs advice, she's glad to have strong friendships with other godly women.

Men appreciate the "earnest counsel" of their friends, as the verse states, but first they tend to do much of their pondering alone. By the time a man goes to his friend for advice, he's usually got a bottom line in mind and is just seeking a nod of assurance.

Women, on the other hand, tend to ponder out loud, with the earnest counsel of friends coming back to them in the same way—out loud. If a man had to hear all that thinking, he'd likely go nuts.

If you're married or dating and consider it selfish to spend time developing godly female friendships, think again. You need it. Your man needs it. And God likens such friendships to pleasant perfume and incense. ✷ *Trish*

Today's Prayer

Lord, thank You so much for my girlfriends. Thank You for their godly counsel when I need it. Please bless them and help me provide godly counsel to them in return. Amen.

Act Now!

Dear children, let us not love with words or tongue,
but with actions and in truth.

1 JOHN 3:18

This verse reminds us that God's action, God's truth, is always given as a side dish to love.

A famous Christian recently came out and said she was leaving the church. Not Christianity, not Jesus, but the church. She said she didn't fit in and couldn't find a connection with God's people. After a heated argument among a group of Christians, she was cast off, dismissed, as not a real believer. Someone who denied God's commands could not be a Christian.

What bothered me about this conversation was that it was so easy for a group of solid Christians to cast off this person, though she was still a young Christian. For her, the church hadn't been a warm place. I wonder how many have that same truth...and yet we condemn them, as if there's no truth in their statements. But if we're honest with ourselves, have we welcomed everyone who walks through our church doors? Have we made it a point to *make* everyone welcome there, rather than to *say* that everyone is welcome there?

What ended up being a scriptural argument that ended in self-satisfaction did not (to me, anyway) take into account that a woman who claimed to love Jesus and called Him her Savior had been summarily shut out because she had not lived up to their ideals of a Christian. If that were my son or daughter, could I so easily dismiss them? Could I decide that their walk with the Lord was over because they'd broken this "rule"?

Christ laid down His life for her...for me. Don't we owe it to Jesus to look into the matter within our own hearts before we condemn another? Where this woman's faith is, I can't be sure—it's not for me to know. Those who obey His commands live in Him and He in them. I don't know about you, but there are times during each and every day when I couldn't claim this. It's why I continually struggle to listen to that still, small voice even when it feels overwhelmingly impossible.

To be famous while becoming a Christian must be incredibly difficult. I remember all the idiotic things I said in my youthful zeal of becoming a Christian. What would it be like to have all that recorded for YouTube history?

Before you decide someone else's walk, will you take the time to look at your own? Will you treat that person with love and not hate—which, by the way, God calls murder, and He goes on to say that no murderer has eternal life in Him (1 John 3:15). It's not a small matter. ✳ *Kristin*

Today's Prayer

Dear Jesus, help me to be kind and to love in action
and in deed today. Help me to sow love where there is none.
Help me to pass on Your love where I don't feel it.
May the sweet scent of Your truth be on my lips. Amen.

He Crowns the Year

You crown the year with your bounty,
and your carts overflow with abundance.

PSALM 65:11

Not long after I was diagnosed with ovarian cancer, reality began to set in...and fear followed. Disability insurance would provide only half of my regular income over the period of time away from work for surgeries and treatment. Would I be able to keep the lights on, the telephone at the ready? Would there be food in the refrigerator?

A local friend in whom I'd confided sent me a card with today's Scripture in it, and she scribbled a note on the bottom. "He promises. You can count on it."

But how? The hysterectomy took its toll, and recovery was excruciatingly slow over the next six weeks. As I prepared to begin five weeks of daily radiation therapy, my slashed income started to catch up to me. I looked up at my friend's card where I'd placed it in my office, and I shook my head. "You promised, Lord," I reminded Him.

Back then, author Loree Lough was a valued writer bud whom I'd only met via the Internet. She and I frequently chatted on IM, and we'd developed quite a budding friendship. She emailed and called me many times during my recovery. Then one afternoon in the mail came an envelope from her address, and inside was a check for $100.

But wait! There were three more envelopes in the stack of mail, each of them from longtime friends in different states across the country. $100, $75, $50. The next day it was more of the same. It turned out that the friend who'd given me that Scripture card had privately contacted ten of the friends she'd most often heard me speak about and asked them to help in any way they were led to keep me above water until I came out on the other side, cancer-free. As a result, each and every time I flipped a switch, lo and behold, the lights went on. With the push of a button, *voila!* A dial tone. And my refrigerator stayed stocked throughout my treatment and beyond with whatever bland food I could manage to keep down.

Ever since that time, whenever I come across today's Scripture, I smile and think of that first envelope I opened from Loree. Since that time, Loree and I have collaborated on one book and brainstormed on I don't know how many others, and we've finally met in person. Our friendship has morphed into a sort of sisterhood that began with the arrival of that first check and the sweet little note she attached about how much she had come to love me. Loree and my other friends who came through for me at that time were God's hands to crown my year with His goodness, and I'll never forget them (or Him!) for it. ✳ *Sandie*

Today's Prayer

Thank You, Lord, for the many ways and people
You use to exhibit your goodness. Amen.

Heavenly Music

"The Lord your God is with you, he is mighty to save.
He will take great delight in you, he will quiet you with his love,
he will rejoice over you with singing."

ZEPHANIAH 3:17

The crowd scrunched shoulder-to-shoulder in the pews, each person eager to catch a glimpse of his or her child in the children's program. With the cameras and videos charged and ready, the children trudged toward the platform, a child here and there stopping the flow to wave wildly at a relative in the audience.

Dressed in their Sunday-best and giving eager smiles, the children belted out tunes of praise to their God. Some stared at their shoes. Some hid behind the person in front of them. Some scratched, nodded, waved, or stared at their neighbors. Yet nothing diminished the audience's adoration for the young performers.

Off-key melodies brought smiles and apparent pride to the listeners. Spellbound and enraptured with the budding artists, the audience's adulation escalated with every number, and by concert's end an uproarious applause broke out in their midst.

As I ponder those moments where my husband and I sat in awe and delight of our own children's musical offerings, I can't help but think of today's Scripture and how we live our lives in much the same way.

The melody of our lives is a little off-key. Fears assail. We try to hide our failures, making one excuse after another. Sometimes life's challenges make us wonder how we will get through another day. We wave at God for assurance that He is there. We question how He can love us when we are unlovable. We struggle to understand how He can meet our needs when they are so great—when we feel certain there is no way out or that all is lost.

Life bulldozes pain into our tranquil world. Life turns things upside down. Life brings questions and doubts. Life brings fear.

Ah, but God is in control. Much like a parent watching a child in a church program, He watches over our lives with a love we can't begin to comprehend. He loves us when we mess up, sing off-key, get distracted, or forget our words. He understands our pain, our fears, our questions, and our doubts. And you know what? He loves us still. Like the warm embrace of a mother holding her baby, His love wraps around us and carries us through the good and the bad days of life. He never leaves us.

Did you get that? *Never. Leaves. Us.*

So the next time you're faced with a challenging day, know that our Father longs to quiet you with His love and rejoice over you with singing! ✳ *Diann*

Today's Prayer

Father, help me to remember that no matter
the melody of my life, You are the Composer
of my days and You offer a song of love
in the midst of my chaos.

Kick Me When I'm Down

God is our refuge and strength, an ever-present help in trouble.

PSALM 46:1

When my husband walked through the door at noon on a weekday more than a couple of decades ago, I didn't have to ask if something was wrong. Instead, my question was, "What happened?" He tipped his head toward our two daughters, our unspoken language for letting me know we'd discuss whatever it was later.

Once the kids had finished their lunch and were outside playing, my husband and I sat down at the kitchen table. "I lost my job," he said. "The company cleaned house, and they got rid of most of the people in my position." My shoulders sagged. We'd only been in our house for a year—not enough time to build equity to pay a real-estate commission, so we couldn't sell. And just a few months earlier my mother's health had failed, and she was two states over, living in a persistent vegetative state. I felt as though someone had kicked me after I'd already fallen.

My husband and I discussed options. He'd always been a good provider, but the economy was in a downturn and options were limited. I was a stay-at-home mom of two toddlers. I didn't want to put my children into day care, but I was willing to do whatever was needed to help the family. For a time, I had to scrape money from the spare-change jar to keep food on the table while my husband got another job and worked an obscene number of hours to pay the mortgage. It was never easy, but when one of us got down, the other was able to rise up and do a little extra.

There's no doubt in my mind that the Lord was the source of our strength during that very difficult time. We had many sleepless nights, wondering how we'd be able to provide for our children without losing our sanity or some of the precious moments of their childhood. My wonderful mother-in-law, Bobbie, stepped in and traveled with me to visit my mother until my mother died. If it weren't for Bobbie, making the trip to see my mom would have been nearly impossible with two toddlers who didn't understand what was going on.

I can't say *anything* during that time was easy, but with His strength, we persevered. During the times we felt as though we may fall, He scooped us up. If it weren't for our faith in the Lord, our family might have wound up being a statistic. He didn't promise that we'd be able to keep our house, but somehow we managed to live there until we were ready to move. Life has been smoother lately, but after that rough time, I know that with God's strength, I can face whatever challenges come before me. ✳ *Debby*

Today's Prayer

Dear Lord, I come before You in gratitude for the
strength You have provided. Without You, the difficulties
of this life would overshadow the joys. Amen.

You Can't Argue Alone

Do not answer a fool according to his folly,
or you will be like him yourself.

P R O V E R B S   2 6 : 4

*A*re you big on arguing? Combativeness can be contagious. I was at my most argumentative when I dated a man who was practically a caricature of the "fiery Latino." He argued passionately about everything from who was the best pickup basketball player (after *every single game* he played) to which restaurant made the best shrimp scampi. It was exhausting.

One thing I've noticed as I've aged is that I don't get into arguments as easily as I used to, despite the strengthening of my core beliefs (about important things, not basketball and shrimp). When I was younger, it seemed so important that my points were at least understood, if not embraced. I was infected with last-word-itis.

After I became a Christian, an unsaved friend of mine constantly instigated arguments with me about a particular moral issue. She knew where Christians generally stood on the issue, so she assumed (correctly) that I stood there as well. She, of course, stood on the other side of the matter. She was forever sending me newspaper articles to back up her argument and turning our otherwise-entertaining conversations to the debate.

I felt an obligation, as a Christian, to engage her when she did this—to help her understand the truth. I didn't think she was a fool, but because of the Lord's Word, I knew that her stance was worldly folly. It wasn't until I asked one of my pastors for advice about a particular point that he adjusted my view of the problem.

"I don't mean to belittle your friend," he said, "but you know that verse about not casting pearls before swine? It sounds as if your friend isn't seeking clarity about your Christian stance on this matter. She's just trying to denigrate your beliefs. She's not seeking understanding; she's seeking to destroy."

I knew what I believed and what she believed. My friend knew the same. What were we accomplishing by constantly rehashing an argument neither of us would concede? I chose to refuse further debate with her on the subject. Proving myself right wasn't important, and God was going to have to convince her of the truth since I couldn't.

She wasn't happy about it, but she had to drop the assault because I was unwilling to play "my role." Sometimes it's best to just step away from the argument, ma'am. Just step away and pray. I like this anonymous saying: "When you're arguing with a fool, make sure he isn't doing the same thing." ✳ Trish

Today's Prayer

Lord, I pray I'll always be able to account for my belief
in You and Your promises. But please help me to know the
difference between a true seeker and a mere mocker. Fill me
with the Holy Spirit, so I might guide the former and
dismiss the latter to Your instruction. Amen.

Kristin Billerbeck is a best-selling author of over thirty novels and novellas. She is a Christy-award nominee, a two-time American Christian Fiction Writer Book of the Year winner, and the author of *What a Girl Wants*. When not writing, Kristin is generally hovering over her four children, hanging out in Silicon Valley coffee shops, and praying that it will be a good hair day. Visit her website at www.KristinBillerbeck.com, or her popular blog at GirlyGirl.typepad.com.

Sandra D. Bricker says she hasn't had a good hair day in twenty years. With eleven novels in print and five more slated for publication through 2012, she has carved out a niche for herself as an award-winning author of "Laugh-Out-Loud" comedy for the inspirational market. Sandie was an entertainment publicist in Hollywood for 15+ years for some of daytime television's hottest stars. When her mother became ill in Florida, she left Los Angeles to provide care...and begin her writing career! Visit Sandie's website at www.SandraDBricker.com, or her weekly blog at SandraDBricker.blogspot.com.

Diann Hunt writes romantic comedy and humorous women's fiction. She admits to seeing the world from a slightly different angle than most, and she will do just about anything (within reason) for chocolate. Since 2001, Diann has published three novellas and seventeen novels. Her books have finaled in numerous contests, and she has won the American Christian Fiction Writer's prestigious Book of the Year award in her genre. Diann and her real-life hero-husband make their home in Indiana. Visit her website at www.DiannHunt.com.

 **Debby Mayne** grew up in a military family that moved often throughout her childhood. She was born in Alaska and has lived in Mississippi, Tennessee, Oregon, Florida, Hawaii, and Japan. Debby has published more than 25 books and novellas, approximately 400 short stories and print articles, hundreds of online articles, and a slew of devotions for busy women. To learn more about Debby, visit her website at www.DebbyMayne.com.

 Award-winning novelist **Trish Perry** has written seven inspirational romantic comedies for Harvest House Publishers and Summerside Press. She has served as a columnist and as a newsletter editor over the years, as well as a 1980s stockbroker and a board member of the Capital Christian Writers organization in Washington, D.C. She is a member of American Christian Fiction Writers and Romance Writers of America, and she holds a degree in Psychology. Trish invites you to visit her website at www.TrishPerry.com.